CW00739525

Predictions for the 21st Century:

How Mankind Will Change

and Some Will Simply Fade Away

Dennis Marx

Copyright © 2015 Dennis Marx

All rights reserved.

ISBN-13: 978-1517584320
ISBN-10: 1517584329:

DEDICATION

To Bernard Mandeville and the Fable of the Bees

CONTENTS

Acknowledgement   i

1 **Predictions for the 21st Century**   1

2 **A Survey of Demographics**   5

3 **Why Has Fertility Collapsed?**   47

4 **Human Evolution**   57

5 **Evolutionary Emotions**   65

6 **Economy & Culture**   75

7 **Investing in the 21st Century**   93

8 **Final Notes**   97

9 **Afterword and References**   99

ACKNOWLEDGMENTS

I freely stole ideas from every author mentioned, but the blame falls on me alone

PREDICTIONS FOR THE 21ˢᵀ CENTURY

After the end of the second millennium AD, history appeared to have taken a pause. There was talk of the end of history. The United States seemed to stand dominant across the world stage and everything appeared to be moving toward peace, cooperation and prosperity.

Just 15 years later, the end of the millennia pause has turned into nothing more than a phantom. The United States has gone through 15 years of gross mismanagement from the US federal government in Washington. The old industrialized nations are fading of their own accord. China appears to be rising and trending increasingly toward belligerence in its newfound prosperity and Russia is moving desperately to recapture past glories imagined through a Soviet colored lens. History has begun anew.

These predictions for the 21ˢᵗ century are not primarily to do with politics. They are merely a look at what can be said using a few, little appreciated tools. The first tool is that of demographic projections. The next is a vision of the human being and human behavior from the point of view of the biologist. Evolutionary requirements have impacted the nature of human behavior. Developing an understanding of this evolutionary psychology can inform predictions of how humans behave on the average. The result of the examination is a few specific, but limited, predictions of what the world will continue to see and other general but broad predictions of the near future.

Survey of Countries

In the first 15 years of the new millennium, human fertility in the world has come crashing down everywhere. Fertility is so low that in most of the world there aren't enough births to replace the existing population. Further, in almost all the rest of the world fertility will drop below the rate needed for replacement in 5 to 15 years. Given current trends, the final holdouts, mostly in sub-Saharan Africa, are very likely to follow that same path within another generation

The average age of the world population will grow throughout the 21st century and beyond. In the near term, the above 50 population will increase while the younger, below 50 population, will remain steady. After 2050, the younger population will be in a steady decline and the over 50 population will become a greater and greater percentage of the human race.

As this occurs, the absolute level of poverty will decline, traditional societies will disappear and every country will move, almost universally, into the modern world. The new prosperity will not be caused by the population decline. The population decline will be caused by the absorption of traditional societies into the modern world as they begin to prosper.

Evolutionary Biology

Current popular thinking is that humans evolved in some distant past and have been genetically stable for tens of thousands of years. Logic and science say otherwise. Mankind is undergoing accelerated evolution due to the rapidly changing environment they inhabit, and all the while the modern world continues to change at an ever-increasing pace. A pace that is outstripping human evolution. In biological terms, human beings have become genetically unfit to survive in their current environment. The modern world has left them behind.

The result is dropping fertility, primarily from the emotional aspects of human behavior. These are not functioning in the modern world in the sense that, in many cases, they are not leading to offspring. In many more situations they are not leading to as many offspring as the same emotional features would have produced in previous environments.

Humans' *emotional computer* previously led to a high level of fertility. In an oversimplification, human quest for status in traditional and historical social organizations, combined with a strong male sex drive resulted in a high rate of fertility. In the modern world the quest for status has become a global, rather than local event and more and more often is leading to infertile sex. Human desires are increasingly moving humans toward delayed marriage and limited offspring.

Evolutionary Calculus and Human Emotions

The range of human emotions is vast and enormous volumes in fields as disparate as psychology, sociology and economics among many others, have been devoted to examining human behavior. Examining humans through an evolutionary lens is more recent, but it can solve some longstanding economic conundrums and predict future cultural developments.

Human shame and guilt became less of a driving force as people became more mobile in the modern society. The mobility allowed people to reinvent themselves. Things have changed again, however. In a world connected by social media the past will become increasingly difficult to shake, and shame will again become a much stronger force.

Economists model human behavior by assuming that they wish to maximize their wealth and are naturally risk adverse to various degrees. However, using this model, certain behaviors cannot be explained. Specifically, gambling, and especially lotteries do not fit into their models and neither do financial bubbles. These behaviors can be explained, however, by assuming that humans are seeking status rather than wealth. The status goal is tied to genetic fitness because status increased current and future progeny in Homo Sapiens' *evolutionary environment*.

Human violence between groups, including instances of genocide, was also nurtured in the *evolutionary environment*. This is a natural way for one group to promote their gene pool at the expense of another group. The vilification between opposing groups will continue, it will still be accompanied by violence and will lead to more instances of genocide, especially in an age of advanced weaponry.

Economy and Culture

The worldwide economy will continue to improve at the highest and lowest levels. Technological improvements will filter down to the poorest of the poor. This will suck them into the modern world, creating a more unified cultural outlook. It will also increase dissatisfaction even as wealth and material conditions improve. Meanwhile, culturally, mankind will enter a new era. The percentage of older people and seniors will reach levels of the population unheard of anytime in history. This will create an *Ossified Society* as resistance to change increases. There will be a series of *Invisible Generations*. Younger generations in the 21st century will have less visibility, fewer opportunities to rise in existing hierarchies and less influence in popular culture.

A SURVEY OF DEMOGRAPHICS

Fertility is collapsing across the entire world and will continue to collapse for the foreseeable future. The population of the world is quickly becoming older as well. The total population over 50 will almost double in the next 35 years. Then, even as the overall population begins to shrink, the over 50 population will continue to grow.

A survey was performed using US Census projections of the world population on a country-by-country level. The US Census data contained historical population data and created a projection of the population for each country through the year 2050.

The US Census data on the 18 most populous countries in the world, countries that contain almost 70% of the world population, show fertility quickly falling or, in a few cases, where fertility has been below replacement for decades, rising slightly, but remaining well below replacement. These 18 countries are broadly representative of their regions in the world. Other countries in each region have similar fertility and demographics.

In all the countries examined and in the world as a whole, the population over 50 almost doubles while the under 50 population remains stagnant. In the second half of the 21st century, the over 50 population will continue to grow modestly, while the under 50 population shrinks.

Per capita GDP has grown steadily in most of the countries in this survey. Inequality grew as well. There are substantial differences between the GDP growth rates in these countries. Poverty and subsistence economies are disappearing, however, as even the poorest countries have sustained per capita GDP growth rates above anything seen prior to the 19th century. The poorer people of the world are becoming richer on an absolute basis.

China

China will be one of the dominant countries of the 21st century, though less so than current popular culture would project. The Chinese population will remain stable to the middle of the 21st century, but then start falling at an accelerating rate. China's miracle economy will also begin hitting internal, structural ceilings that will strongly curtail per capita GDP growth within the next 5 to 8 years.

China's Current Demographics

China's female fertility is 25% below replacement and has been so for more than 20 years. The US Census projects that the overall population will remain fairly stable over the next 35 years, dropping by 60 million from 1.36 Billion now to 1.3 billion in 2050.

The population of females under 50 in China is 466 million today and is projected to drop by 33% to 320 million in 2050. This is from a peak of 499 million in 1999.

China's infamous One Child Policy is exacerbating some of the drop. A cultural preference for sons combined with the One Child Policy has resulted in significantly more young Chinese males than females. The typical biological ratio of males to females at birth is 1.05 males to females. China's ratio is now 1.11 and peaked at over 1.18 in 2005. This has resulted in an excess of young males.

Currently, the number of Chinese males 15 to 29 is 164 million compared to 147 million Chinese females in the same age group. In 2020, this is projected to be 140 million males to 122 females. In 2025, the ratio is projected to be 126 million to 109 million. In 2030 the ratio will reach 122 million males to 106 million females. These numbers require no prediction of future fertility and only project the current younger Chinese population's mortality and mobility.

	Chinese males 15-29 in Millions	Chinese Females 15-29 in Millions
2015	164	147
2020	140	122
2025	126	109
2030	122	106

Figure 1. Chinese Male and Female Populations, Ages 15-29, Projected to 2030

As of 2015, China's population over age 50 is 387 million. This is projected to rise to 634 million in 2050. The under age 50 population is 974 million and that is projected to drop to 667 million by 2050.

	Chinese Over Age 50 in Millions	Chinese Under Age 50 in Millions
2015	387	974
2050	634	667
Change	247	(307)

Figure 2. Chinese Over and Under 50 in 2015 and 2050

China's Future

A Note on Reviewing the Projections

The US Census used 2 questionable assumptions in their projection. The first is the assumption that the sex ratio at birth would normalize to 1.07 males to females almost immediately. One reason for this is a relaxation of the One Child Policy. The ratio is more likely to stabilize near its current level of 1.11. This is in line with India and also with Vietnam, which has a similar culture. This difference will overstate the number of young women in 2050 by roughly 2%, or 6 million.

The second assumption overstates the future Chinese population. China's total fertility rate has been gently rising with the easing of the One Child Policy, going from 1.52 to 1.56 in 10 years. The US Census assumes a linear increase of the total fertility rate through 2050 to 1.7. The factors that have led to a collapsing female fertility across the world are present in China to an even greater extent than elsewhere. Wealth and female education has expanded. The awareness of the wide world, the status of females, birth control and pornography are ubiquitous. They exist in China as much or more than across the rest of the globe.

The fertility might continue to creep up, but is likely to stabilize or even retreat past the next 10 years. This will result in a projection that overstates the number of Chinese under the age of 25. In 2050, the Chinese population below the age of 25 might be reduced by as much as 12 million people below the current projection.

Population Projections

Population projections have multiple moving parts. Without big events, like the black plague, mortality is fairly stable. Migrations between countries are less stable, but usually have a smaller impact than mortality for any one country. The variations in the current trends of migration should produce only modest future errors in a population projection.

Fertility is usually fairly stable over short periods, but can vary greatly over a decade or so. For example, fertility in the US during the great depression fell dramatically from that of the roaring twenties and then came back strongly during the 1950's baby boom.

Some external events can strongly influence the nature of fertility. One example of these are the development of inexpensive ultrasounds combined with sex-selected abortions. This has had an impact in Indian fertility. A second example is the Chinese One Child Policy. In both cases, these have upset the typical male to female birth ratio.

The at birth sex ratio is normally very stable and near 1.05 males to females. Currently, the One Child Policy in China and sex selected abortions in India have upset the standard biological Birth ratio. The typical 1.05 rate is off by 5% to 10% in both countries.

Mortality is fairly stable and predictable, fertility has more variability. The result is that the first part of a population projection, the part based upon mortality, is very accurate. The second part of a population projection however, the part based upon fertility, is less accurate.

Mortality and migration make up the first part of a population projection. In one year, a highly predictable number of people will die and a usually smaller number and fairly predictable number will migrate in and out of a country. The population will also, of course, be one year older. In the 35 years between 2015 and 2050, the prediction of mortality and migration will be fairly accurate, but all those people alive today will be 35 years older.

The second part of the population projection relies on accurately projecting fertility as well as mortality and migration. The estimate of the people that will be 34 years old in 2050 requires an estimate of the children born in 2016 and that cohort's mortality and migration for the next 34 years. That requires an estimate of the females in their childbearing years as of 2016 and their fertility.

In the short run, the number of births will be fairly stable and similar to the current year. Over time there will be less certainty and it will drift from the current fertility. Each year projected forward adds another year estimated using projected fertility. The variations become greater and the projection becomes less accurate. The younger the age, the greater the variability. The projected population of 34 year olds in 2050 will have less certainty than the population of 35 year olds. The certainty of the population projection of 5 year olds will be much less certain than the projection of 34 year olds.

The US Census prediction of the Chinese population over 35 in 2050 is very reliable. The prediction of the population under 35 in 2050 is much less so. The population prediction of the number of children under 5 is the least sure.

Future Population

Young females and their fertility are the source of a population's growth. Specifically, the gross female reproduction rate is the number of females born to a female over her childbearing years at current fertility levels. This determines whether a population will increase or decrease. If this rate is below 1, there are not enough females born to replace those growing past their child bearing years.

In a very real sense, China's population will have dropped by 32% from 2015 to 2050. This is because it's fertile female population, all females under 50, will have dropped 32% from 466 million in 2015 to 320 million in 2050. If the alternate scenario occurs, the reduction will be more. That is, if the male to female sex ratio does not revert to 1.07 and the fertility rate does not continue a straight-line increase. In this alternate case, the Chinese population of fertile females will have fallen 37%. Which would be a 41% drop from the under 50 female population peak of 499 million experienced in 1999.

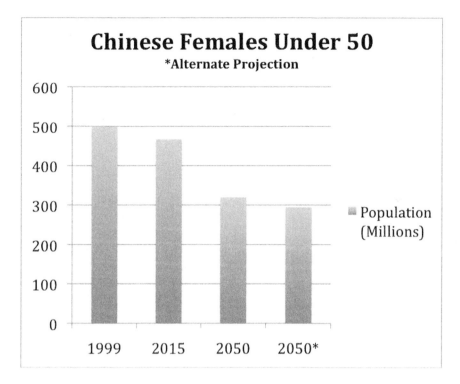

Figure 3. Chinese Women in Their Childbearing Years and Younger

China's population will begin falling gently within ten years. After another two generations, the population will fall by more than 33%. If fertility remains stable, as is likely for a few generations, the trend will accelerate.

Future Gender Mismatch

For the foreseeable future China will have 15% more young men than young women. The falling population will exacerbate the impact of the gender imbalance. There are a few paths that can result from the imbalance, but overall, Chinese men will be driven to take greater risks. There will be some combination of social unrest, emigration and increased competition. The Chinese government appears to want to channel any unrest into xenophobia and possible war in order to ease domestic strife.

Economy

The Chinese economy has been the talk of the world for the last 15 years. GDP has gone from $1.2 Trillion in 2000 to over $10 Trillion today. Per Capita GDP has gone from $1,000 in 2000 to $8,000 in 2015. This growth is generally associated with the liberalization of the economy to a more capitalistic, free market. However the move has been only partial, and there are still many government run corporations, a lot of central industrial planning as well as a great deal of corruption. These will likely put a cap on the recent unrestrained growth that will begin to limit the Chinese economy at a modest per capita GNP.

This situation is not unprecedented. In living memory there have been a few instances where rapid growth of a country occurred. In each case, there were fears expressed that the country would continue the growth indefinitely and pose a danger to world peace. Calls were made that the United States needed to copy the country in order to keep up. As an example consider these 3 other times when a country had extraordinary growth, concerns were expressed, and there were calls for the US to implement a centralized industrial policy governed from Washington.

Russia

From 1946 though 1955 Russia experienced an average per capita growth rate of 6.4%. In fact, it was this growth and Soviet hubris that had Khrushchev telling US diplomats that the communists "Will bury you". From 1955 through 1988, before any impacts of the Soviet collapse were felt, the Soviet economies average annual per capita growth was well below 2%.

Germany

From 1946 through 1959 the German per capita income grew at an average rate of over 9%. This again led to calls that the US economy would do better with a modest industrial policy led by intelligent people out of Washington. Since 1960, the average German per capita growth rate has been 2.5%

Japan

Throughout much of the 1980's, Japan was presented as an economic miracle, that needed to be imitated through an industrial policy directed from Washington, and as a threat to the world order. Japan had achieved average annual per capita growth of almost 6% from 1946 through 1988. More recently, this has not been an issue. Japanese per capita growth over 20 years from 1988 to 2007, the start of the great recession, averaged only 1%.

In all three cases, the exceptional growth was initiated at a disaster point, WWII. In each case, per capita GDP grew quickly up to the point that internal structural constraints, such as the size of the government, inefficient management structures and available technology curtailed the growth. Of course the US is currently implementing greater limitations on its ultimate achievable per capita GDP and has been doing that for a couple dozen years, and that has been limiting the US economic growth.

The same will happen in China. The disaster in China was communism. Once that was largely removed, the Chinese people were able to grow and prosper. The level of corruption and government ownership, taxation and central control is a relatively new mix, but the top per capita GDP will be reached. It will be significantly better than the Soviet Union and worse than Japan. A reasonable guess, is that the structural impediments in the Chinese economy will cause the GDP per capita to top out somewhere between $12,000 and $16,000 in current US dollars, or 5 to 8 more years of extraordinary growth.

In the long run, China's population decline will cause severe strain on the economy. In 2050, almost half the population will be dependents either over 65 or less than 20 and almost half the remaining workforce will be between 50 and 65.

India

China's high male to female birth ratio is well known. What is less well known is that India has a male to female birth ratio comparable to China's. India has also had a significant drop in fertility. The drop is less than China's however, and India still has a fertility rate above replacement. The fertility will continue to drop, and the drop will occur at a faster rate than the US Census has projected. Because of the high proportion of younger people in India's population, however, India's population will continue to increase until roughly the end of the 21st century.

India's Current Demographics

India female fertility is 2.48 children per female. That is the *Total Fertility Rate or TFR*. This is a drop from 3.45, in 1990, 25 years ago. The male to female sex ratio at birth has been steady at 1.12 for 25 years. These combined result in a female reproduction rate of 1.17. That is the *Gross Reproduction Rate Per Woman* or the number of females that the average female will bear over her lifetime at current fertility rates. The population of India in 2050 is projected to reach 1.66 billion from 1.25 billion in 2015, and the number of females under 50 is projected to reach 535 million from 488 million today.

There are 174 million Indian males today between the ages of 15 and 29 and 155 million females aged 15 to 29. In 2020 the number of males is expected to rise to 181 million and females to rise to 160 million. By 2025 the numbers are expected to reach 184 million males and 162 million females. In 2030 the numbers will remain the same at 184 million males and 162 million females. Sex ratio differences are as large or larger in India today than they currently are in China and have been unbalanced longer. This will likely cause some of the same problems for India, as they will for China. In the short run, however, India's increasing population will mitigate the depth of the problem in India.

	Indian Males 15-29 in Millions	Indian Females 15-29 in Millions
2015	174	155
2020	181	160
2025	184	162
2030	184	162

Figure 4. Indian Male and Female Populations, Ages 15-29, Projected to 2030

Currently there are 225 million Indians 50 or older and 1.03 billion Indians under 50. In 2050, the population below 50 is projected by the US Census to increase slightly to 1.12 billion. The US Census projection has the over 50 population more than doubling to 540 million by 2050, however.

	Indians Over Age 50 In Millions	Indians Under Age 50 In Millions
2015	225	1,030
2050	540	1,120
Change	315	90

Based On US Census Projection

Figure 5. Indians Over and Under 50 in 2015 and 2050

India's Future

Issues With the US Census Projection

A glaring problem with the US Census projection is the assumption that the at birth sex ratio of 1.12, that has existed for 25 years will change to 1.06 within 10 years. There is no 'One Child Policy' in India. The 1.12 male to female birth ratio is entirely due to parents that seek out ultrasounds to selectively abort girl babies. Sex selected abortion is already illegal in India, so it is unlikely, without a major cultural shift, that this practice changes.

The fertility projection also is highly suspect. Fertility has fallen steadily for 25 years. However, the projection includes only modest fertility drops in the next 35 years. The US Census predicts India's fertility will only just reach replacement levels by 2050.

Based upon results in similar Asia nations, a more significant drop should be used. All the events that have triggered strong fertility drops across the world are quickly entering India. Female education and awareness is on the rise. The Internet is widely available and a vibrant middle class is growing. A total fertility rate near 1.75 in 2050 is much more likely than the US Census projection of 2.05.

India's Gender Imbalance

India's gender imbalance it not as well recognized as China's. It came into being starting in the 90's when widespread availability of ultrasounds made determining the baby's gender early during pregnancy possible for the masses of Indians. The issues Indians' face are the same that the Chinese will face. Males will begin to be greater risk takers. Channeling this for the good of India will be a challenge. One mitigating factor in India, however, is that the population is still rising. Since males often marry younger women, especially males that are marrying late, they will have an increasing pool of younger women as potential mates. At least they will have this option until the fertility rates drop in the next 10 to 15 years.

Population Projection

Under US Census assumptions, the population of India will grow 33% by 2050. The fertile female segment of the population will only increase by 10%, however. If the projection is adjusted to have a realistic birth sex ratio and to have a fertility decrease in line with current world standards these numbers will be altered. In this alternate projection, there will be 30 million less males under the age of 35 and 46 million less females under the age of 35. In this alternate case, the total population will have increased only 26% by 2050, the total increase in the below age 50 population will be less than 1%, and the fertile female population increase will vanish.

Economy

In the 45 years after World War II, India implemented highly statist, socialist economic policies and consequently had a per capital GDP growth rate of 1.6%. Since 1991, India began to liberalize their economy and have experienced sustained growth rates over 5%. India still has less than half of China's per capita GDP, however. It is difficult to estimate the point at which India's central bureaucracy, corruption and state control will put a limit on their economic growth. Unless they backtrack on their economic liberalization, however, economic growth is likely to continue at a strong pace. In the late 2020's and early 2030's expect the news to be inundated with surprise at the Indian miracle along with the normal predictions about how India is going to own the world.

United States

The United States is the third most populous country in the world. It is also significantly different demographically due to a long history of diverse immigration and a high level of continued immigration. A quick discussion of US demographics is below. A more detailed examination is separated out in a later chapter. The later chapter focuses on some current US controversies regarding the relative growth of various population segments and the implications of those differences.

United States Demographics

The US fertility has been fairly flat, at replacement, for some time. However, the overall fertility has dropped slightly during the latest recession. Current US total female fertility is 2.01 and the at birth sex ratio is 1.05. The female replacement stands at 98%. The US Census has total female fertility dropping slightly over the next 35 years.

The total US population is expected to increase from 321 million today to 400 million in 2050. Females under 50 are projected to rise from 104 million today to 120 million in 2050. There are currently 119 million Americans over 50 and 215 under 50. In 2050, the US Census projects that there will be 154 million people over 50 and 246 million under 50.

America's Future

In every country, there are subtle sub-population dynamics, and America is no exception. These elements usually have interesting implications over the long run. The text will not discuss these issues, except for the case of the United States. This discussion will be provided in a later section.

The US population will grow 25% over the next 35 years. The fertile female segment of the population will only grow 15%, however. Almost half the population increase is expected to come from immigrants.

Much is made of the retirement of the baby boomers. In the United States the current, 2015, population above the age of 65 is 15% of the total US population. In 2050, it will be 21% of the total. This is a minor issue by international standards. In China, for instance, the current percent of population over 65 is 10% and it is expected to increase to 27% by 2050. For China, that is just before the peak of their population begins retiring, so the problem for the Chinese, will only be getting worse. In the United States, retirements will be at a steady state.

China, India and the United States have almost 3 billion of the 7 plus billion people on the planet. Each of these three countries is fairly unique demographically. China and India have gender ratio issues, though each achieved them in different ways. The United States is the world magnet for immigrants.

For the next 15 countries in this survey, there are patterns and similarities by region that emerge. The 18 countries in the survey contain more than 2/3rds the world's total population. The remaining countries, with a little less than 33% of the population, have demographic characteristics that are very similar to these next 15 in this survey.

Eastern Europe and other former Soviet occupied countries have similar demographics to Russia. Western European countries look similar to Germany. South American Countries are similar to Mexico or Brazil. Middle Eastern Countries follow Turkey or Iran. Most Sub-Saharan African countries are similar to Nigeria and Ethiopia.

Indonesia

Indonesia is the fourth most populous country in the world. It has experienced a substantial drop in fertility over the last 35 years. Indonesia will have less than replacement fertility before 2020. Indonesia's sophisticated, modern population is over 50% urbanized and rapidly increasing it urbanization rate. Indonesia's fertility is likely to continue it's descent over the next 35 years.

Indonesian Demographics

The Indonesian total fertility rate has dropped from 4.37 in 1980 to slightly above replacement at 2.14. The gross reproduction rate for women is 1.05. Indonesia has a long history of the standard biological 1.05 male to female birth ratio. The US Census projects that the Indonesian population will increase from 256 million today to 300 million in 2050. However the number of fertile females are expected to drop 9%, to 91 million in 2050 from 100 million in 2015.

Today's over 50 population is 51 million, with 205 million under 50. In 2050, 35 years hence, Indonesia is expected to have 113 million people over 50 and 187 million younger than 50. At the same time, the projection is for fertility to drop a little less than 20% from its current value. At that point Indonesia will be at 85% replacement.

	Indonesians Over Age 50 In Millions	Indonesians Under Age 50 In Millions
2015	51	205
2050	113	187
Change	62	(18)
Based On US Census Projection		

Figure 6. Indonesians Over and Under 50 in 2015 and 2050

Third World Fertility Considerations

The US Census fertility projection for Indonesia over the next 35 years is reasonable in many ways. It projects a continued drop in fertility, but at a slower, more conservative rate than Indonesia has gone through in last 35 years. In the last 35 years, the fertility rate has dropped to a little more than half its previous value. Future fertility is difficult to predict. However, the model used by the US Census has most likely overstated Indonesian fertility between 2015 and 2050.

Japanese, Western European and Former Soviet Block countries have experienced fertility drops down to female replacement levels of 60%. The assumptions the US Census is applying to developing nations come from a lack of understanding of root causes of the worldwide fertility collapse.

The assumption is that countries formerly counted among the third world cannot experience either the first world industrial type fertility or the fertility experienced in former Soviet occupied countries. This is the residual of commonly held assumptions on the nature of fertility between educated, industrial countries with wealthy people, and poorer, less educated people in countries with more traditional, backward, lifestyles.

Traditional lifestyles have disappeared to a greater extent than is currently recognized. The implicit assumptions about the drivers of fertility are in many cases due to correlations, not causation. The whole world is experiencing a collapse in fertility simultaneously. The old assumptions of the causes of the collapse are driving analysts to project fertility in developing countries at much higher levels than the conditions warrant.

Indonesian Population

While the Indonesian population is projected to increase 15% over the next 35 years, the basis for future population growth after 2050, young females under 50 will drop 9%. The population peak in 2050 will be in the 45 to 49 year old age range. At that point, the 45 to 49 age cohort is projected to be 25% larger than the population of children 0 to 4. Adjusting the projection to account for a lower level of fertility, indicates that there will be 6 million less Indonesians in 2050 than the US Census projections. A little more than 3 million less men under 35 and 3 million less girls under 35. The drop in females still in or before their childbearing years would be 12%, instead of 9%.

Indonesian Economy

For an extended period, Indonesia's per capita GDP has been rising at a 3% annual rate. The increasing burden of an older population is unlikely to hamper growth until late in the 21st century, so an average of at least 3% per capita GDP growth for many years is likely. At these growth rates the per capita GDP is unlikely to face structural constraints from the Indonesian government or culture for well over 10-15 years.

Brazil

The depths of the Brazilian fertility collapse to well below replacement will surprise many, since Brazil was predicted to be ground zero in the population explosion. The Brazilian population will peak in the first half of this century, likely even earlier than currently predicted.

Brazilian Demographics

Brazil is another country where the elite consensus was that it would see a booming population increase, only to have its fertility collapse. In 1980 Brazilian women were having an average of over 5 children each. In 2015 that number is 1.77 or 86% of replacement.

Brazil's population is expected to increase from 204 million in 2015 to 232 million in 2050, a 14% increase. The fertile female population will decline, however, from 79 million today to 68 million in 2050, a 14% decrease. The population above 50 is currently 46 million and the younger population is 159 million. In 2050 this will change dramatically to 95 million Brazilians above 50 and 137 million Brazilians younger than 50. The population peak will be at slightly below the age of 50. The population above 65 will triple from under 16 million today to almost 50 million in 2050.

Brazilian Population Projection

The issues with the US Census projection of the Brazilian population are the same as the ones of the Indonesian projection, only more obvious. The total fertility in Brazil has dropped over 56% in the last 35 years, and the US Census has the fertility dropping just 4% more in the next 35 years. Fertility will most likely fall farther and faster than this projection. A more likely projection will have 10 million fewer Brazilians under 35 in 2050. This would lead to only a 9% increase in total population of Brazil between 2015 and 2050 to 222 million, and a 20% drop in the fertile female population from 79 million in 2015 to 63 million in 2050.

Whether the drop in fertile female population is 14% as in the US Census projection or 20% as in the alternate projection, the long-term consequences are continuing and accelerating population decline in Brazil through the 21st century and beyond. Because the drop in fertility came later, the peak population of Brazil will follow that of China by 20 years. Because the fertility appears to be dropping more slowly, the exponential decline in population will not be as fast, but Brazil's population will reach a peak near 2045 and a decline of 15 to 20 percent will already be baked into Brazil's future, as a 33% drop will be baked into China's. The population drops will compound generation after generation until the fertility reverses.

Economy

The Brazilian economy has lagged behind many of its neighbors and has experienced a lower per capita GDP growth rate, about 1.5% than any major South American country other than Venezuela. Brazil has excellent long-term opportunities if the Brazilian government would stop implementing policies that impede the country's growth.

Pakistan

Pakistan is an example of a country that has a reputation as backward with a low education rate for women and less freedom. Yet it has experienced a breath-taking reduction in fertility. Even so, the US Census predicts that the fertility fall will nearly halt immediately, falling less in the next 35 years than it has fallen in the last 7 or 8 years. This projection reflects the prejudice of Pakistan's reputation and fails to recognize one of the highest urbanization rates in the world. Pakistan is no longer the traditional, rural society it was 35 years ago. It is increasingly an urbanized, wired society and it will continue to act like one.

Pakistani Demographics

Pakistan's fertility is currently well above replacement, at 2.75 children per female. This, however, is down from almost seven children per female as late as 1980. This represents an astonishing drop of over 4 children per female in not much more than a single generation. After dropping precipitously for 30 years, the US Census projects a modest drop in fertility over the next 35 years to a level just barely below replacement.

Pakistani population is expected to increase almost 100 million in the next 35 years, going from 199 million in 2015 to 291 million in 2050, a 46% increase. The fertile female segment of the Pakistani population is set to increase from 83 million in 2015 to 100 million in 2050. This is a 20% increase. Currently, less than 1 of 7 people in Pakistan are over the age of 50. There are 27 million Pakistanis over 50 today, in 2015, and 172 million Pakistanis under the age of 50. In 2050, that ratio will be close to 1 in 3 with 87 million Pakistanis over 50 and 204 million under 50.

Pakistani Population Projection

The Pakistani US Census fertility assumptions are suspect for the same reasons the assumptions made for other 3rd world countries are, as discussed above. Fertility assumptions that reach replacement in the next 10 years and fall well below replacement after that would reduce the 2050 population by 20 million, indicating a 36% overall increase. The fertile female growth would only be 8% in this scenario.

Pakistani fertility has been falling rapidly from a very high number. However, a very high proportion of Pakistan's population are females still in their childbearing years. Pakistani females under 50, those still fertile or that have yet to begin their childbearing years, represent 31% of the total population. In comparison, 22% of the Chinese population are females in the same age group. This population will be the driving force behind the Pakistani population increase for the duration of this projection period. The falling fertility, however, will have a very strong influence on the Pakistani population in the later half of this century and will lead the Pakistani population ultimately lower.

Pakistan has spent the last 35 years running headlong into the modern world. It has a young fertile population, and that will translate into many years of population growth. But it has entered into the modern world and will have fertility rates reflecting that move. Over the next 50 years the Pakistani population will age and sometime in the late part of the 21st century it's population will begin to decline in line with the rest of the world.

Nigeria

Nigeria has the largest population of the West African nations. The high fertility and the population projections are typical for the region. Along with the rest of sub-Saharan Africa, this is where most of the worldwide population growth in the next 35 years is expected to occur. The fertility is falling, but from very high levels. The fall in fertility is significant and on going.

Nigerian Demographics

Sub Saharan Africa is the area of the world where the population boom is predicted to continue unabated and Nigeria is the prime example. The total population of Sub Saharan Africa is 923 million as of 2015 and is projected to more than double to 1.9 Billion by 2050. Nigeria, the most populous country in Sub Sahara Africa has a population of 182 million and represents nearly 20% of this total in 2015. Nigeria is projected to more than double its current population, to 391 million, by 2050, growing slightly faster than the region as a whole. Nigeria is a good proxy for Sub-Saharan Africa.

Nigerian fertility is very high, but even in Nigeria fertility has dropped considerably. In 1980, Nigerian women were averaging 7.04 children each. By 2015, that number has dropped to 5.19. The US Census predicts the rate will drop further in the next 35 years to 3.28.

The population is projected to increase 115% in the next 35 years. The female population under 50 is projected to grow from 80 million to 165 million, a 106% increase. The number of Nigerian females under age 30 is projected to drop from 34% percent of the current population, or 62 million, to 30% of the 2050 population, or 118 million. This is a 90% increase in females under 30, however. The population growth is slowing down, but Nigeria's population will, in reasonable scenarios, continue to increase spectacularly through this century.

Nigeria's Future

It is possible that Nigeria's fertility, along with the rest of the Sub Sahara, will collapse more quickly and come in line with the rest of the world.

The trend in Sub-Saharan Africa is toward lower fertility. Correctly predicting how fast fertility will decline there and how low it will go is unlikely. It is very possible that the region will have 1 out of every 3 or 4 people on earth by 2050. Much more than the 1 out of every 8 people it holds today.

Economy

Nigeria, and the region as a whole, has had a 1% annual growth in GDP per capita. It is likely that this rate will continue for decades. This is a dismal rate for modern times, but it will move Africa into the modern world sufficiently to impact future fertility rates negatively.

Bangladesh

Bangladesh is one of the poorer countries in the world. It is also, excluding a couple of island countries and a few city-states, the most densely populated. Just 30 years ago, it was predicted that Bangladesh would be mired in poverty and crowded beyond comprehension. Since then, the fertility has fallen to just above replacement, while the economy has produced 3% per capita GDP growth for the past 25 years.

Bangladeshi Demographics

Bangladeshi fertility is modestly above replacement at 2.4 children per female. The rate has dropped from 5.66 in 1985, 30 years ago. This puts female replacement at 118%. The sex ratio at birth is 1.04 males per female. The population is projected to reach 250 million in 2050 from its current level of 169 million in 2015. The number of females under 50 is expected to rise to 84 million in 2050 from 73 million today. The percentage of population above 50 is expected to double to over 33% from 16% today.

Bangladeshi Projection

The US Census has projected that Bangladesh will have future fertility similar to India and Pakistan. This projection will likely be overstated as it is in those cases. A reasonable estimate indicates that the US Census overstates the 2050 Bangladeshi population by about 16 million. This adjustment in fertility will remove almost all of the projected increase in the population of females in and before their childbearing years.

Economy

The Bangladesh economy has shown per capita GDP growth averaging over 3% for the last 25 years. This growth is likely to continue. Per capita income is still very low by world standards. Bangladesh per capita income is a little more than 33% of India's. The increases have also been considerably slower than India's, so some acceleration in growth is possible.

Russia

The Russian population is currently falling and it will continue to fall throughout this century with the population decrease accelerating as the century progresses. Russia projections are somewhat different than those in most countries. They do not have the older age groups increasing as fast as is the case in Japan and Western Europe. This is due to higher mortality rates of Russian males. The mortality difference is due to poor health with a significant impact from alcoholism.

Russian Demographics

Russia fertility has been well under replacement for many years. At the turn of the millennium, Russia was at just a bit over 50% replacement. They have risen in fertility since then and are now running at 78% replacement. The population is expected to drop by 8% to 130 million in 2050 from 142 million in 2015. The females with childbearing years in front of them will drop 24%, from 46 million today to 35 million in 2050. In 2015, 50 million Russians are over 50 and 92 million are under 50, a little more than 1 in 3. By 2050, it is projected that 59 million Russians will be over 50 and 71 million will be under 50.

Russian Projection

The US Census projects Russian fertility to remain at its current 1.6 level for the next 35 years. This is a reasonable estimate, though the fertility level might increase as well. Either way, the Russian population will continue to fall past 2050. The most likely scenarios have the Russian population continuing to fall for 100 years after 2050.

A stable, strong, and confident Russia would be a positive element in global peace. The current rapidly dropping population, along with a history of devastating invasion, is adding to Russian insecurity. Hopefully, arrangements can be made in the future to reverse the animosity existent between Russia and the West as well as between Russia and her near neighbors stemming from cold war suspicions. It is not likely to happen soon, especially after the repeated missteps on the part of the US in the 25 years since the dissolution of the Soviet Empire.

Japan

The Japanese fertility has fallen farther and for longer than any other country in this survey. Japanese fertility has long been well under replacement. The Japanese population will fall dramatically during the 21st century and continue to fall in the 22nd century as well.

Japanese Demographics

Japan's fertility has been below replacement for decades and Japan is projected to continue to have low fertility for many decades more. Currently, the Japanese total fertility rate is at 1.4 and the gross replacement rate of women is at 68%. The population of 127 million today is expected to drop to 107 million by 2050. The population of females under 50 is expected to drop by more than a third, from 34 million today to 22 million in 2050. Currently there are 20% more Japanese under 50 than over 50. In 2050 this is expected to reverse, with a third more Japanese over 50 than under.

Japanese Projection

Female fertility has been rising gently over the last 10 years and is projected to continue to rise gently for the next 35 years, but all through this period the fertility is projected to remain well below that required for population replacement. The impact on the Japanese population will be dramatic. In 1990 there were 43.7 million Japanese males under the age of 50 and 42.5 million females under 50. The 42.5 million females represented 34% of the Japanese population in 1990.

Over the 60 years following 1990 those numbers are projected to fall almost in half. There will be 23.5 million males and 22 million females under 50. At the projected 2050 fertility rates, those 22 million females will give birth to 24 million babies after 2050, 11.5 million of which are females. Those 11.5 million will in turn have 8 million female babies and the 8 million will have 5 million and so on for each generation, unless the Japanese fertility has a dramatic turn around.

At the point a little after the end of the 21st century, when the Japanese population has reached 5 million females of childbearing years, there will still be a fairly large Japanese population, but most will be older than 50. If not for the older population, for instance, if the population profile were similar to that of 1990, the total population, based upon 5 million females, would be roughly 16 million, or less than the population of Japan in 1500.

The Mathematics of the Japanese population is an example of where the world population appears to be heading. The fertility numbers the world is seeing will have a modest impact on the overall size of the population in the short run. However, the population base that is responsible for creating future generations, females in their childbearing years, will be falling dramatically. That population segment, females under 50, ultimately determines the future of the overall population. Japanese females in their childbearing years are experiencing exponential declines as powerful as the exponential growth of population observed in the 19th and 20th centuries, and this will have as great an impact on the future as that exponential growth did.

Mexico

Mexico looms large in the popular culture as a land with great food, poverty and high fertility. While Mexican per capita GDP growth greatly exceeded the US per capita GDP growth in the last 6 years, the biggest surprise to many will be Mexico's collapsing fertility. In 2015, Mexican fertility was just above replacement and falling quickly.

Mexican Demographics

Mexican fertility is just a little above replacement and has been falling steadily. The fertility stands at 2.27 in 2015, which is a drop from 3.33 twenty-five years ago in 1990. Female replacement stands at 111%. Mexico's 2015 population is 122 million and is expected to reach 151 million in 2050. There are 23 million Mexicans over 50, which is a little less than 20% of the population. There are 99 million under 50 in 2015. In 2050, the percent of the population over 50 is projected to grow to 36%. The projection puts 55 million over 50 and 96 million under 50. The number of females under 50 is projected to drop 2%, from 49 million today to 48 million in 2050.

Mexican Projection

Mexican fertility is projected to drop steadily, if modestly over the next 35 years. From 2.27 today to 1.7 in 2050. The drop is significantly slower than the last 25 years, but is a more realistic drop than other third world projections, such as those for India and Pakistan. The projection points to a significant contraction in the Mexican population in the 100 years following 2050. As an illustration, if Mexico continued at the fertility predicted for 2050, these 48 million women in their childbearing years would replace the 96 million Mexicans under 50 with only 68 million people and the women under 50 category would drop over 30% to 33 million.

The fertility and economics of Mexico is typical of many Latin American countries. Many are experiencing moderate growth and collapsing fertility. While Mexican fertility is currently still above replacement, it has not been above replacement after historical net migration. Though, as prospects have fallen for economic growth over the last 6 years in the US due to new US federal government policies, net migration from Mexico may have reversed. This situation may be semi-permanent as the continuing collapse of Mexican fertility greatly reduces the pool of younger Mexicans interested in immigrating.

Philippines

The Philippines has shown decreasing fertility, but has defied the experience of most other East Asian countries and still has fertility well above replacement. A reasonable projection should place the Philippines below replacement within the next 20 years. Per Capita economic growth has also been below other East Asian countries but may very well improve.

Philippine Demographics

Fertility is currently 3.02, down from 4.21 in 1990. Female replacement is at 147%. The population is expected to increase significantly, from 110 million today to 172 million in 2050, an increase of 56%. The population of fertile females is expected to rise from 46 million today to 62 million in 2050, an increase of 35%. Currently, less than 15% of the population is over 50. There are 16 million of the 110 million Filipinos that are over 50 and 94 million younger than 50. In 2050 the percentage of the over 50 cohort is expected to almost double to 27% of the total population. The actual number will almost triple, with 46 million Filipinos over 50 compared to 115 million under 50.

Philippine Projection

Fertility has fallen by 1.2 children per female in the last 25 years and is projected to drop 0.8 children per female in the next 35. This is a plausible scenario, but given the experience across Eastern Asia, the projection is most likely to be overstating the future fertility. The population rise over the next 35 years is projected to be 56%. With an alternate fertility projection, the population will have 11 million fewer Filipinos under 35 than the US Census projection. That is a 46% projected increase in total population. Under the US Census projection, the childbearing and younger female population is projected to rise 35%, from 46 million to 62 million. Under the alternate scenario, the increase is only 24%.

Economy

The Philippines has had per capita GDP growth of 1.6% over the last 25 years. This is likely to continue for the foreseeable future. The higher average age should improve productivity at these levels.

Vietnam

Vietnamese culture and genetics have been greatly influenced by China over millennia. Vietnamese demographics are currently also similar to the Chinese, even without the introduction of a one-child policy. In the short run, the Vietnamese will experience solid economic gains. In the 21st century they will face a quickly aging population, however. In the last half of the 21st century, the population of Vietnam will begin a long-term slide.

Vietnamese Demographics

Vietnamese demographics have several similarities to Chinese demographics. Fertility is low. It has fallen from 3.62 in 1990 to below replacement at 1.83 in 2015. The birth sex ratio is currently 1.11 males per female, also in line with China's. The population is currently 94 million and is projected to increase to 111 million in 2050. There are currently 37 million females in their childbearing years or younger and that number is expected to drop to 32 million by 2050. The population older than 50 is currently 18 million, with 76 million under 50. In 2050, this is projected to rise to 46 million above 50 while the population under age 50 will drop to 65 million.

Vietnamese Projection

Fertility was cut in half over the last 25 years. The US Census projection predicts that it will drop 7% in the next 35. While the overall population will increase and is projected to grow 18% in the next 35 years, the fertile female population will drop 12%. With an alternative scenario, the projected growth in the population will drop slightly to 13% and the drop in the fertile female population from 2015 to 2050 will be 18%. The over 50 segment of the Vietnamese population is currently at 19%. This is expected to grow to 41% by 2050.

Economy

Economic growth has been very high, with per capita GDP increases at almost 6% for 25 years. The growth began from a very low starting point when Vietnam began liberalizing their economy after years of communism and it likely still has significant room to continue improvements before reaching internal limits. The relative population over 50 can support continued growth in the near term, but will reach levels after 2050 that strongly restrict increased growth in per capita GDP.

Ethiopia

Ethiopian fertility has fallen modestly, but is still at the stratospheric level of over 5 children per woman. Ethiopia's fertility is fairly representative of their part of Eastern sub-Saharan Africa. Ethiopia is both one of the poorest nations and a nation of fast economic growth. This is because

Ethiopia is still recovering from the devastation caused by a communist interlude under Mengistu. The communist interlude lasted until 1991, when the Soviet Union began collapsing.

Ethiopian Demographics

Ethiopian fertility in 2015 is 5.15 children per female. This is a drop from 6.83 in 1990. The female replacement ratio is 254%. The population is expected to grow from 99 million today to 228 million in 2050. The number of females in and before childbearing age is expected to increase to 97 million from 45 million today. The population over 50 in Ethiopia is 9 million today versus 90 million under 50 and is expected to rise to 34 million in 2050, with 194 million under 50.

Ethiopian Projection

Ethiopian fertility has been dropping modestly since 1990. The US Census projects the fertility to continue dropping as fast after 2015. Even so, Ethiopia will still be above replacement in 2050. The population is expected to increase 130% in 35 years and the fertile female population is expected to increase 116% during that period. Currently, the percentage of the population that are females in and before childbearing age is 45%, a very large portion by modern standards. Every one in eleven Ethiopians is currently over 50 in 2015. In 2050, that will increase to more than 1 in 7.

Economy

Ethiopia is one of the poorest areas of the world. The per capita GDP is a quarter India's per capita GDP, and that is after 11 years of spectacular growth, that almost quadrupled the size of the economy. If Ethiopia continues this path of growth, it is likely to begin to face the modern world. If that happens, the US Census projections will have significantly overstated future fertility. If Ethiopia experiences an extended period of peace and continues economic liberalization, a fertility collapse like that experienced in the rest of the world is a likely scenario.

Egypt

Egypt is the most populous country in the Middle East. While Egyptian fertility is still well above replacement, it is falling along with the entire Middle East. A reasonable projection would put Egypt below replacement in less than 20 years.

Egyptian Demographics

Current Egyptian fertility is 2.83, down over the last 15 years from 3.46 in 2000. The female replacement ratio is at 138%. The population is projected to increase to 137 million in 2050 from 88 million in 2015. The number of females in and before their childbearing years is projected to increase to 48 million in 2050 from 36 million in 2015. There are currently 14 million Egyptians over 50 and 74 million Egyptians under 50. This is projected to change to 40 million over 50 in 2050 and 98 million below 50.

Egyptian Projection

The US Census projects Egyptian fertility to decrease as much in the next 35 years as it has in the last 15. The current projection has the population increasing 56% and the fertile female population increasing 33%. An alternate scenario with lowered fertility shows a 34% increase in population from 2015 to 2050 and a 7% increase in women of childbearing years.

Economy

Egypt's per capita GDP has been growing slowly over the last 25 years. Until the crash in 2009, it averaged about 2% annual growth. Though recently that has fallen. The growth at these levels is likely to continue for an extended time under the current government. The GDP per capita is roughly on par with India, but growing much more slowly.

Germany

German Fertility has been far below replacement for decades. An influx of immigrants has sustained some population growth, but Germany has passed a population peak and has declined in population since a little after the new millennium began. This will continue. The population will continue to fall, slowly at first, but the fall will accelerate in the last half of the century.

German Demographics

German fertility is 1.44, with female replacement at 0.7. The current population is 81 million and that is expected to drop to 72 by 2050. The number of fertile females is projected to drop to 18 million in 2050, from 22 million in 2015. The population over 50 in Germany is currently 36 million with 45 million younger than 50. In 2050 the population over 50 is projected to drop to 35 million and the population under 50 is expected to drop to 37 million

German Projection

German fertility has been below replacement for decades, but has been rising slowly in the last 20 years. The US Census predicts than the fertility will continue to rise gently, but remain well under replacement through 2050. Germany's current population is projected to drop by almost 14 million, but the US Census predicts that more than 4 million immigrants will enter Germany to partially offset that loss.

German population demographics are similar to Western Europe as a whole. England, and France have lower current populations, but modestly better fertility. Though they also are still below replacement. Italy and Spain have fertility very close to Germany's rates and are going to experience similar population declines over the rest of the 21st century.

Iran

Iran has had one of the most sudden fertility collapses. As a result, it is having a sharp move toward an older population. The population will continue to grow through 2050, though the productive members of the society will begin to fade toward the end of that period. In the last half of this century, Iran will enter a sustained period of population decline

Female fertility in Iran is below replacement. Fertility has fallen precipitously from 5.6 children per woman as late as 1990 to 1.83 in 2015. The US Census projects that the fertility drop has stopped. They project that the fertility will be almost flat after 2015. Female replacement is at 90%. The sex ratio at birth is 1.05 males to females.

The population is projected to grow 22%, from 82 million in 2015 to 100 million in 2050. The fertile female population is projected to drop by 12% however, going from 33 million in 2015 to 29 million in 2050. The above 50 population is projected to more than triple. It will go from 13 million in 2015 to 41 million in 2050. Meanwhile, the under 50 population will drop 13%, starting from 68 million today and falling to 59 million in 2050.

The fertility after 2015 will likely be lower than the US Census projection. This will have a modest impact of a few percent of the younger age population by 2050. It will have significant longer-term impacts, however. It is most likely that the population of females in the childbearing years will continue to fall and that this will accelerate.

Turkey

Turkish demographics are fairly common in the Middle East. It is multi-ethnic, with a Kurdish population in the Eastern, more rural, segment of the country. The Kurdish fertility exceeds the more urban Turks in the western section. The Turkish population is growing while the fertility is falling and headed below replacement.

Turkey's total fertility rate has dropped from 3.22 in 1990 to replacement level 2.05 in 2015. Female replacement is at 100%. The US Census expects a continued fall in fertility to 1.73 by 2050. The total population is projected to increase from 83 million in 2015 to 101 million in 2050. In 2015, there are 17 million Turks over 50 and 65 million under 50. The number of Turks over 50 is expected to more than double to 39 million in 2050. The population under 50 will drop to 62 million in 2050.

Fertility has been falling steadily and the US Census projects that it will continue to fall at a slower pace. The percent of the population over 50 is expected to almost double from 20% to 40% by 2050. The overall population is expected to increase by 22%, though the US Census projects the fertile female population to decrease 3%.

Turkey is currently experiencing a gentler decline in fertility than most of the rest of the world. Even so the population is aging rapidly. Just 25 years ago the percentage of over 50 population was less than 14%. Since then, it increased 50%, to 21% in 2015 and will grow to almost 40% by 2050. It is projected to continue to grow, both in real terms and as a percentage of the Turkish population, for some time after that.

All the rest

This survey of 18 countries represents 5 billion of the Earth's 7 plus billion people. The next 81 most populous countries have a total of 2 billion people. These 81 have similar demographics to the survey countries that are in their region.

Of these, 26 are Sub Saharan African and are similar in demographics to Nigeria or Ethiopia. These have a total population in 2015 of 631 million. They have slightly lower fertility than Nigeria and Ethiopia, the Sub-Saharan countries in this survey, but overall are still well above replacement fertility.

Another 12 countries in the next 81 most populous countries are in Western Europe. These have a total of 326 million people and are similar overall to Germany. The largest 2 are Great Briton and France. These two countries combined have 131 million people and higher fertility than Germany, but are still well below replacement. The next 2 countries by population in Europe are Italy and Spain with 110 million total population combined and fertility very similar to Germany.

Latin America is the third largest contributor to this group, with a 261 million population. These 13 countries have demographics similar to Brazil or Mexico. Of the top 4, Colombia, Argentina and Peru are more similar to Mexico in economics and Venezuela is more like Brazil.

The Far East, Middle East, South East Asia and former Soviet Block countries represent 753 million people and have demographics and economics similar to the survey countries that are from their regions.

Summary

For almost 50 years popular opinion, driven by sociologists, economist and armchair environmentalists have been warning of a population explosion and instead, the opposite is occurring. The human population of the Earth is in the early stages of an implosion.

This was unforeseen and is unexplained. Since the implosion began in the industrialized world, the early, facile, explanations have centered upon the differences between these industrialized societies and the developing world as to what made for slow population growth. Using that model, the population growth seen in third world countries was predicted to march forward unabated. Ultimately, a catastrophe was predicted as per capita income fell and food production and infrastructure failed to keep pace with the exploding population.

A new look at this is required. Instead of considering what needs to be done to curb population growth, the world needs more thought directed toward how to handle aging and declining populations, especially in the developing nations.

As for predicting where human fertility is heading, it turns out that biology and evolution can answer these puzzles where sociologists, political scientists and environmentalists have failed so dismally. Evolutionary psychology has explanations as to why human fertility is collapsing. This new perspective leads to new predictions, not just on fertility and population growth, but on what will happen broadly worldwide as the collapse continues. It provides insight about how far the collapse will spread, and how fast and how long it will last.

A World of Old People

Virtually every country in the world is experiencing collapsing fertility. There are a few exceptions, those countries that have already experienced a collapse in fertility and are slowly increasing their fertility to levels just a little below replacement. It appears that fertility will continue in this pattern for every nation on the planet. The peak of the world population will occur before 2050 and then for a few decades the total population will gently recede. Then the world's population decline will accelerate. Fertility will rebound over time, though the rebound is more likely to look similar to the fertility rebound in Russia and Germany rather than a robust baby boom.

Even the period of gently dropping population beginning in 35 years is deceiving in it's impact. In every country, the population over 50, as a percentage of the total population will boom. The decades where the population is slowly changing will be a period where the percentage of the population over 50 is increasing quickly, while the population under 50 is falling. That crashing younger population will be locking in future decades of population decreases.

For example, in China the over 50 population will rise almost 250 million, while the under 50 population will fall by over 300 million. There are 5 Chinese under 50 for every 2 Chinese older than 50 today. The ratio will move to 1 to 1 by 2050. In India, the US Census has the over 50 population increasing over 300 million from 2015 to 2050 and the ratio of over 50 to under 50 going from 1 in 4.5 to 1 in 2. In Germany the ratio goes from the current level of 5 in 9 to a ratio of 5 in 6. Even in Sub Sahara Africa the ratio is increasing. There are more than 9 people under 50 for everyone older than 50 in Nigeria today. According to the US Census projection, with its overstated fertility, that will change to 1 in 6 by 2050.

What Will a Society of Old People Be Like?

A society and culture composed of the old rather than the young is a new phenomenon and will be contemplated in a later chapter. A society composed almost entirely of the young is nothing new. In Ethiopia 90 million people were under 50 and 9 million were over. That is typical for most of human history.

One probable economic outcome is that capital will become cheap and labor will become dear. Wealth is accumulated over a person's lifetime. Those funds are invested and spent down over time. With a very high and growing percentage of people with a lifetime of accumulated wealth, returns will drop, especially on low risk investments. On the flip side, labor becoming dear will encourage automation.

Another outcome is that risk taking will be reduced. This will also be seen in investments, where lower risk investments will be chosen over higher risk options. It might also be prevalent in governance as well, where older people will chose stability and resist change, even change that is necessary.

USA

The US has experienced significant legal and illegal immigration over the last 30 years. Overall, the immigration has been and will continue to be good for the country. The popular media has promoted a fear of this immigration by portraying the new immigrants as a separate and insular group. The media have painted a picture of the immigrants greater fertility swamping the existing citizens, taking over the countries institutions and flooding the country's generous social and welfare programs.

While there are many issues to be concerned about, especially in the last 6 years of meager economic growth, many of the fears are unfounded. One legitimate issue is competition for jobs with the native population, since the influx of immigrants has been shown to be suppressing wage increases. It is also true that there is also a tendency of welfare and social service agencies to attempt to capture immigrants as clients by encouraging these new immigrants to avail themselves of generous benefits. On the other hand, immigrant fertility, especially Hispanic fertility, is well below that imagined and immigrant assimilation is occurring quickly.

Immigrant fertility is greater than native fertility, but overall it is falling fast. The fertility of second generation Hispanics moves quickly in line with the current population and the overall Hispanic fertility, across all the America's, north and south, is also falling.

Immigrants, specifically Hispanics and Asians are also intermarrying with the broad US population quickly. In a few generations, the differences will be similar to the Italians and Poles and Irish. It will become a part of the proud ethnic heritage of Americans.

There is a great deal of discussion and concern that the new waves of immigrants will create a permanent political realignment. Progressive groups are hoping for and working toward a continued alienation of Asians and Hispanics in order to exploit them for political advantage. This will become increasingly difficult to achieve in the environment of intermarriage now seen and the growing number, and growing acceptance, of multi-ethnic children.

Hispanics

Currently, a popular paradigm in the US media is a focus on an expanding Hispanic population and how it will come to dominate the US. This has had significant political fallout. There are calls to change platforms and policies in order to court the Hispanic voting block. While there are many issues on immigration that need to be dealt with, demographics and population projections can shine considerable light on these issues.

Southern and Eastern Europeans

The United States has been through something like this before. The US had a large influx of Southern Europeans, Eastern Europeans and Irish some 100 to 150 years ago. These groups were highly suspect and initially maintained tight ethnic enclaves. They did tend to vote for one group over another. These patterns dissipated over time. Intermarriage became acceptable, then commonplace, and finally so ubiquitous that it is invisible. The voting patterns initially so striking, have disappeared as the groups became assimilated.

That is one model Hispanics might follow. The alternate model is that Hispanics become a permanent underclass and don't assimilate. The hope of many is that in this case, that they develop a strong antipathy for the majority population and continue to vote with a strong bias against them.

There is strong evidence for assimilation in the Hispanic population and some against it. History is in favor of assimilation. Almost all groups have eventually assimilated. Some evidence of this shows up in marriage statistics. Recent numbers show that over 25% of Hispanics are marrying outside, mostly to Caucasians. With intermarriage that high, there will be strong family ties. Strong family ties will go beyond husbands and wives and mothers and fathers to include brothers and sisters-in-law, nieces and nephews and grandparents. It will be difficult to maintain strong antipathy between these groups, and encourage the necessary alienation to keep Hispanics separate, even if outside groups continue to push discrimination stories and a range of other divisive themes.

A second narrative that has been pushed is that Hispanic groups have high fertility rates. This has been true in the past, but the differences have lessened and are likely to continue falling. The main reason is the quickly falling fertility occurring across Latin America. The second piece of evidence is that there has consistently been a tendency for second and later generation Hispanics to have fertility very similar to US natives.

Where Babies Come From?

A common perspective in US popular culture currently being pushed is that high fertility in minority groups will cause them to dominate the US population later in this century. This is often pushed in a political context, where this evolution will result in the future dominance of the Democratic Party and progressive policies. This is the variation on the Hispanic narrative discussed above. There are several issues with this narrative. First, there is the issue of assimilation. Mixed marriages are common and growing in numbers. Over 25% of Hispanics and more than 25% of Asians enter mixed marriages. Of all marriages in recent years 15% have been multi-ethnic. By far the largest of these are Hispanic or Asian with Caucasian. These rates are likely to increase.

A second, often overlooked issue with the standard narrative is that levels of multi-ethnic children are high, undercounted and growing quickly. In most cases, these children are categorized as minorities and even often placed in a standard ethic category for simplicity, usually as a minority. It is far from clear if this is how these people view themselves. What is clear, is that as this process continues, minority will be an ever more tenuous social construct. It will in many instances, cease to have meaning; at least in the way it is used today.

Another factor in US fertility is religion. The Amish, Orthodox Jews, Mormons and Evangelical Christians have above replacement fertility. In some cases, they have well above replacement fertility. It is not surprising that the fertility of these groups decrease with their involvement with the modern world. The Amish have fertility in the range of 6 children per female, or a 6.0 Total Fertility Rate (TFR). Orthodox Jews have fertility in the 4.0 range. Mormons have a 3.0 TFR and Evangelical Christians are at a 2.3 TFR.

Finally, there is one more impediment to the predicted progressive electoral hegemony. A review of attitudes shows a strong divide in political affiliation between married and single women. Specifically, parents of girls show strong conservative tendencies. There is not enough information to predict the future political impacts from this. There does seem to be a tendency of families with more children to align with conservatives and a tendency for progressive Caucasians to have few children. It is also hard to understand the future political impact of the greater fertility of highly religious populations. Since political affiliation often follows family lines, however, they show a demographic tendency that might be as strong, or stronger than other predicted impacts commonly discussed.

Fear of Hispanic fertility promoted by the popular media is greatly overstated. Hispanic fertility is quickly falling within the United States and in Latin American countries. Simultaneously, the high degree of intermarriage is quickly removing the divide between current immigrants and the native population.

WHY HAS FERTILITY COLLAPSED?

There are endless theories as to why fertility rates fall. Many of the reasons floated are due to economic causes. A large number of the reasons posit social causes and some the loss of faith. A lot of the reasons provided are driven by political consideration and worldview. However, there is one perspective that has not been widely considered, the perspective of science, biology and evolution.

Humans often resist the notion that they are animals, but they are. Humans usually consider the environment they live in as somehow separate from nature, but it isn't. Humans also frequently consider themselves as beyond evolution and that evolution was a process that happened in the past and brought humans to this point and stopped. It didn't stop and it won't stop until humans no longer live and breed.

Humans have been evolving continuously and they are now evolving more than ever before. Homo Sapiens are evolving faster now because there are more mutations than ever before, simply because there are more births than ever before. They are evolving faster now because the environment humans live in, and to a great extent have created, is radically different than any of the environments in mankind's past and it is rapidly changing. Human fertility is failing because humans are just not very well adapted to this current, modern, rapidly changing environment.

Some Reasons Given for the Sharp Human Fertility Drop

There are endless reasons given for lower fertility. A quick look on the Internet will uncover the ones listed below and more. Most of the reasons focus on the longstanding differences between the modern, industrial fertility rates and those of the third world. The standard ones are related to those differences since that was where falling fertility was first noted.

These start with wealth, education, greater urbanization, and loss of traditional cultures, secularization and the reduction in traditional farming societies. There are some offshoots of these arguments, such as children becoming an economic drain rather than an economic benefit, or children no longer being needed to support people in their old age with the introduction of social security type programs. Other culprits are women's increased education and employment, the availability of birth control and abortions. Some point to restrictive employment practices and the lack of family leave. At times economic success leads to low fertility, but then economic hard times reduce fertility in other situations. And finally, some have pointed out that women's position in society has improved, they're marrying later, being given more choices and that sometimes those choices are that they don't want babies, don't want babies yet, or just don't want any more babies than they already have.

Not that this list is exhaustive. It is just a sample of the opinions. Many of these items are correlations, not causes. At one time or another almost every difference between developed nations and undeveloped nations has been given as a reason for lower fertility. Then, when the Soviet Union collapsed every difference between the communist world and the third world, such as a lack of religious belief was floated. Some are truisms, like: the number of children women want has dropped. Some are enablers, like birth control.

All of these reasons for falling fertility are given from the perspective of the sociologist, political scientist, or the economist. The sociologist considers the structures of society like urbanization and secularization. The political scientist considers the expanded rights and choices available to women. The economist determines cost and benefits such as what happens when a support network of children is replaced with social security and free medical care. In other cases, economists consider children as a cost and compare the benefits of children to other uses of capital.

Here is a modest proposal. Instead of these perspectives, consider humans from the perspective of a biologist. Humans evolved for hundreds of thousands of years in a fairly static culture. With the advent of agriculture the environment changed significantly and humans accelerated their evolution to fit better in this new environment. The change in humans' environment accelerated. Humans adapted and evolution accelerated in response.

Evolution can only go so fast. The changes in society have become enormous not just within a lifetime, but also within a generation. The environment humans inhabit has changed too fast for human adaptation to keep up. Given the rate of change, it would be amazing if it could.

Where Do Babies Come From?

The birds do not decide to have babies and neither do the bees. Animals, in general, do not choose to have children. However, they do choose their mates, often very carefully. Humans are supposed to be the exception. Are they? Everyone knows that humans choose to have babies or choose not to. My brother chose to have children. My sister chose not to. Of course humans choose.

Free Will to Choose Not to Have Babies is Not a Likely Adaptation

Evolution selects for traits that promote the creation and nurturing of progeny. It is true that this can lead to very complex behaviors in animals and especially humans, but the complexity only hides the basic fact that the evolutionary selection is always biased toward increasing offspring and to the spreading of the individual's genes. If a trait in a species significantly reduces progeny that trait would quickly go away. If humans had complete free will to choose to have or not to have babies, then any humans who had that trait, and regularly chose not to have babies, would quickly be gone. However, if they only had the one possible choice, to reproduce, it isn't really a choice. It just seems like one.

The Evolutionary Environment

Modern humans are considered to have come into existence around 200,000 years ago. During that period, there were extensive variations in their physical environment. Most humans, however, lived fairly similar, tribal lives until roughly 5,000 to 10,000 years BC. The period prior to 5,000 to 10,000 years BC is considered by many to be human's *evolutionary environment*. This is not to say humans stopped evolving then, they didn't. This period is, however, a useful tool to understand humans and the concept of an *evolutionary environment*.

The *evolutionary environment* for a species is the environment that greatly impacted their evolutionary development. This concept can only be a relative since all creatures evolved gradually from similar creatures and those from others. Consider the polar bear. The evolutionary environment of the polar bear could be considered the Arctic. That has been a stable environment where the polar bear developed specialized traits. It is a concept relative to bears in general or to those traits that Polar Bears have with every other or at least most other bears. To consider those broader traits all bears have, it would be necessary to consider a broader and older evolutionary environment.

The Broken Emotional Computer

Humans are finely tuned, complex, survival machines. Most of the machinery is designed around their biggest threat and their biggest opportunity, other humans. In the simplest model however, they are driven to seek status, find love and friendship and have sex. These combined push humans to procreate. Humans have other emotions, of course, and these are all used as fine-tuning to survive and produce as many progeny as their situation permits. That is how biologists see animals and humans are animals. If someone has traits that impede doing this, then someone else, without those traits impeding them will eventually out produce them. The genes supporting traits that impede increasing offspring will disappear.

Status

There is little argument that humans go to great lengths to seek status. Though strangely the same human will never agree that any action they are taking is to seek status. Success, wealth and fame are all aphrodisiacs. Men that achieve status get extra mating opportunities and through the millennia, this has been a very successful method of increasing progeny.

Status - Chimps

Chimpanzees are humans' closest existing relative. Chimps form hierarchies for both males and females. The alpha male chimp, even if his reign is short, typically produces an outsized progeny due to his frequent mating opportunities. Alpha males maintain their position through support of other chimps. They maintain their position through nurturing relationships with top females and male lieutenants.

Status - Tribes

For the first 200,000 years of modern man's existence, they survived in small, extended, kinship groups. Tribal groups are by their nature fairly egalitarian, but status still supports survival and reproductive fitness. It has been documented that success in war results in well over twice the offspring among the Yanomama. Killing an enemy was the way to increased status. This was likely a typical outcome during this period.

Status in Agrarian Society

In agrarian societies, status became an even greater imperative for survival, especially for males. As power concentrated in political hierarchies, those males at the pinnacles of these hierarchies achieved greater reproductive success and those at the bottom had very little reproductive success. The reproductive success of Genghis Khan is legendary. It has been determined that millions of his heirs exist over the range of his and his successors empire. The agrarian revolution has been shown to have significantly trimmed the human gene pool. It was especially harsh to males, dropping male contributors to the current gene pool to a small fraction of the more egalitarian contributions in the era of hunter gathers

People don't connect obtaining status with increased, fit progeny. Men are not striving for status to have more children. There is a driving emotion to win, be admired and obtain better mates. There is an acknowledged connection with sex, but in today's world of widely available contraception, not always to progeny. Rich and powerful men are more attractive to women. Even though men aren't seeking status directly to obtain more children, in the last 10,000 years, the results are just that. Those men have had significantly more offspring and been able to place those offspring where they too can have an outsized genetic imprint.

Love and Marriage

Men and women fall in love and get married. The intent is to be monogamous. Many men have a tendency to cheat. Women cheat also, but by looking at genetic dispersal of Y-Chromosomes, it appears women cheat far less, at least in terms of getting pregnant with another male's child. Men tend to get much more upset at cheating than women do.

Love is a genetic contract. Women are, mostly unconsciously, agreeing to provide offspring opportunities exclusively in exchange for support raising the offspring. Women are not as upset as men about cheating because they likely have less to lose. Some of the males support might go elsewhere. If the man might leave, that might be a different issue. Men have a much greater genetic reason to be upset. They may end up getting tricked into providing precious survival resources to another man's child.

The Male Sex Drive

In case you were unaware, males have a strong sex drive. It is a source of constant amusement what males will do to have sex, how they will have sex, and with what. Huge industries exist to provide males will access to images, sounds, things, videos, and people where sex can occur without the intent to create children and usually without the possibility of doing so.

The Sex Machine

In a very simplified form, these emotions outlined how the machine worked. Men want power and status. That's an impulse at least as old as our break from Chimpanzees 5 million years ago. It is a very natural part of our make-up. The further up in the hierarchy, the more females will provide sexual access. The further up the hierarchy the male is, the more desirable the females that provide sexual access are and the further up the hierarchy he is, the higher the status of the potential mates are as well. Some females, of lower status or less desirability, may make the exchange without expectations, while higher status females may require a greater commitment or marriage.

Before the modern age, sexual access and the oversized male sex drive would ensure babies would occur. There was no requirement to want children. In many ways they were more of a threat historically than now. Men and women could lose their position with inappropriate liaisons, and women could die. However there were limited ways to not have children, so the children showed up.

This is not to say that in many cultural settings children weren't considered a blessing. Though in many of these societies wanting a child, or six or eight, wasn't really a choice if you followed the natural, cultural rhythms. If you wanted to sustain your current status and not risk losing your position in society you played the game. Women married for status, usually at a very young age. Men married for status and position as well, but sexual access also played a large role. However, once the marriage began, human sexual drive, primarily the strong male sex drive, meant that children were often created early and frequently.

The Broken Emotional Computer

In 2015, male status often comes with extra mating opportunities. Stories of sports stars, actors and even former president's sexual exploits fill the popular media. The male is geared to want sex from these encounters. Children, however, are another matter; they are usually to be avoided. With the options available today, the offspring from these encounters are few and far between. Status is no longer bringing the outsized progeny footprint it once did to high status males.

Marriage is also no longer producing the large number of children it once did. Women are getting married later, and they are exercising choice in the number of children. Status has changed. Access to the wide modern world changes women's perception of their status. The status of being the second wife of the local headman vanishes when a 15-year-old girl is bombarded with images and videos of the wide modern world. Status is a different animal after exposure to the world of pop stars and movie actors.

Women do not necessarily want children. Neither do men. In a traditional society, marriage meant status for women and for men it meant status and sex. This led to children. Today gaining status no longer has to result in children. An estimated 20% of pregnancies are terminated in abortion. This does not include those that never occur because of contraceptive practices. More and more, children in marriage, over the entire world, depend primarily on whether the woman and the man want children.

Men have a strong sexual drive. This is a very basic male trait in virtually every animal species. This trait causes males to go to great lengths to seek out females, to compete and fight for them, and even to risk death for a chance to mate. In many species the females go through a fertile period and advertise this with release of scent and through behavior. In human males, on the other hand, attraction is mostly driven by visual stimuli and then by touch.

Males in 2015 are bombarded with constant sexual stimuli. Visual images on billboards, posters, and labels are often designed to attract and stimulate men. Videos and commercials do so as well. In modern society the bombardment is almost endless. At one time the images were of beautiful women, then the most beautiful women enhanced by lighting and make-up and now with touched up photography and CGI, they are of, literally, impossibly beautiful women.

Meanwhile pornography has become ubiquitous in both the modern society as well as anywhere in the world the Internet can reach and its reach has become extensive. It has been reported that the most sexually restrictive Muslim societies appear to have the greatest consumers of pornography downloads off the Internet. It is not impossible that this constant flow of pornography interrupts normal reproductive sex.

Obtaining a mate is a difficult, time consuming, often humiliating, and expensive endeavor. There are a few high status men where this is not true, but for most men, this is the case. It is possible that in many cases the availability of pornography is an outlet that substitutes for trying to improve status, searching for a suitable and willing partner, or settling for a lower status, less desirable option.

Even with males that have access to sexual partners, the availability of sex videos may alter reproductive patterns. The males may seek mating less. Though they might seek it more as well, but have the sexual encounters focus on non-reproductive sex. Given the level of male sex drive, it is likely that every possible and many impossible sex acts have been tried. Many of these do not result in fertile sex. That being said, it is also possible that familiarity and exposure could whet the appetite.

The Fertility Collapse

Fertility collapsed because mankind was not made for modern society. In the very simple model above people did not want children, but they wanted position in society, power, companionship and sex. The desires and the emotions drove people to actions that only incidentally created children. It is true that some children came from couples that wanted them. Often, however, even those people did not want as many as their cultural environment and their desires drove them to have.

People are complex emotional animals. The description above is an immense simplification of all the variables that make up the human condition. The human environment has always changed, but for the last 10,000 years the human environment has been changing radically, ever since the agrarian revolution. That change in human environment is accelerating dramatically. The complex sets of emotions that have driven humans to procreate are misfiring in this new environment. This is what is driving the fertility collapse and as the modern world invades every culture and every corner of the earth the collapse will spread and accelerate until human evolution turns it around.

Status, Marriage, Sex and Evolution

Many pundits are most comfortable with the concept that humans stopped evolving somewhere between 50,000 and 200,000 years ago. The broad popular consensus is that the humans of 10,000 years ago were interchangeable with those of today. They are not. There is broad genetic evidence that humans have evolved greatly in the last 10,000. Given all the environmental changes, it would be inconceivable that they didn't.

HUMAN EVOLUTION

A common view is that humans aren't evolving or are evolving so slowly as to effectively to have stopped. This is false for a couple of reasons. First, the human environment has gone through radical changes. These include some geographic changes as modern humans expanded across continents as well as experienced wild climate differences through the millennia, but most of these changes have been behavioral and societal changes. Human's drastically changed their societal environment at the time of the agrarian revolution and that change has only accelerated through today. The second reason that mankind has accelerated their evolution is the increasing population. The shear volume of human births has greatly increased the random mutations occurring over the last 10,000 years.

Modern humans are estimated to have come into being roughly 200,000 years ago. At that time, a reasonable guess is that there may have been 50,000 humans. A very rough guess is that the total human population didn't reach a million until 130,000 years later, roughly 70,000 years ago. At which time, modern humans were all Africans. Other archaic human like species existed in Asia and Europe such as Neanderthals and Denisovans, but modern humans hadn't yet left Africa. Then, by 10,000 years ago, modern humans had spread across the planet. The other archaic humans were gone. Neanderthals were gone. Even so, humans had only reached a population of around 4-5 million.

Then, the human environment changed dramatically. Humans, most likely somewhere in the Middle East, began practicing agriculture and domesticating animals. In many ways, humans were not suited to this new environment. They had to work harder to survive. They got sick more often. Their lifespan was shortened. However, the human population density of these groups was much greater than those before them. Roughly 6,000 years ago or 4,000 years before Christ, the human population had reached about 7 million. In 1,000 years, that doubled to 14 million. Then it went to perhaps 27 million in 2,000 BC and then 50 million near 1,000 BC. The population was almost doubling as each millennium passed. Two thousand years ago, the population is estimated to have reached 170 million.

During that 10,000 years before Christ, humans evolved faster than the 200,000 years previous. This occurred for two reasons. First, the environment they were living in was enormously different from their previous evolutionary environment. Second, based upon statistics there were more mutations in that 10,000 years than in the 200,000 previous years.

Evolution occurs in two ways. The first is the introduction of mutations. These are positive, negative or neutral in a given environment. The second is selection. A population will have various genes. These will have been introduced over millennia. The environment will be mostly indifferent to the vast majority of these, but will positively impact a few and negatively impact others. Over time the positive genes will tend to be selected for and slowly come to dominate the population and negative ones will tend to slowly drift away. These will only be tendencies, because the basic nature of the process is random.

The environment humans faced after the beginning of the Agrarian revolution was different in multiple ways. Close proximity to humans and herd animals created new and potent pathogens. In a relatively short time, those pathogens weeded out many genes and selected a few with the right immunities. Diets also changed the fitness criteria for humans. Lactose intolerance, for instance, became an issue when supplies of dairy products became available for everyone past the age of weaning.

The greatest impact, however, was the due to the other humans in the environment. People lived in closer quarters. Previously, a high percentage of males died violent deaths. These numbers went down considerably. The ability to cooperate became more important to survival. The ability to rise in a hierarchy became necessary for survival. Being able to become a member of the elites and sustain your family and offspring there became a quality that provided a much greater genetic footprint than it had in previous, hunter-gatherer societies.

These changes would cause increased selection pressure. The traits mentioned above would be selected for in the agrarian environment, where they had not before. In general, with a radical change in environment, the traits that are positive, negative and neutral are different than they were before. This would cause an increased basis for strong selection. Evolution would accelerate. It would accelerate to better adapt the species to the new agrarian environment.

Mutations are random. A mutation that helps fitness rather than one that provides no benefit or actually harms the recipient is rare. The number of mutations should be roughly proportional to the number of births. The percentage of positive mutations in a stable environment will be small. In a rapidly changing environment positive mutations will still be rare, but should have a higher probability of providing positive attributes than in a stable environment, because the species is no longer fine-tuned to that environment.

Since the number of births between 10,000 BC and 0 AD is about the same as for the 200,000 years previous to that, the number of mutations were roughly the same as well. Since the human environment during that period was undergoing monumental changes, the number of those that improved human fitness for the new environment most likely increased.

It is a strange, almost subliminal assumption in popular modern thinking that the environment is something different from human society. From a biological and evolutional perspective, this is unsupportable. The process of choosing mates, and producing offspring is the most important part of the human evolutionary environment. How people respond to that reproductive environment does define their genetic fitness and the variations of those responses have been and are driving dramatic evolutionary changes in the human population.

The Calculus of Evolution

Just as the assumption that humans have been genetically stable for the period since 10,000 years BC is flawed, so would an assumption that humans have been genetically stable in the last 2,000 years. In the 200 years from 1900 to 2100, there were and are projected to be as many births as occurred in all the 200,000 years prior. As many births means as many mutations will occur as in the 200,000 years prior and it is likely that as many or more of these mutations will provide a positive genetic impact as all those previous mutations over the last 200,000 years.

Humans have been and are evolving at a greater rate than ever before and the evolution is accelerating because of the large number of mutations occurring and because the environment humans live in is radically different than anything that mankind experienced before. This puts into question many of societies closely held assumptions and conceits.

Historical Period

For the same reasons that human evolution was intense during the 10,000 years BC, evolution has been intense in the last 2,000 years. With a higher number of births, there have been a higher number of mutations. With a rapidly changing environment, the human specie's selection of traits will increase to adapt to the new situation. These differences include new pathogens and new diets, but also significantly different societal organizations. There has been a continuous change in how humans live and survive with fewer and fewer living in traditional rural settings and more living in urban settings with more varied urban employments. Today's mankind is genetically different than the Greeks and Romans. They are more resistant to disease and more attractive. People today are likely less violent than humans 2000 years ago, and also more cooperative and more intelligent.

Geographical Evolution Differences

Evolutionary pressures differentiated the populations that lived in different geographical areas as well. In many cases, these populations were under different types of evolutionary pressures, while others were under similar pressures, but adapted differently. Finally, over time these groups, being isolated would have been subject to some level of genetic drift.

Two of the areas of strong environmental differences between geographically separated groups are the diseases they were exposed to and the typical diet eaten. Groups evolving in temperate climates didn't develop resistance to tropical disease. Europeans that entered the tropics in the 16th and into the 19th century had very high mortality from local disease. Sub Saharan Africa was an especially harsh climate in which Europeans were not genetically fit. Similarly, the introduction of old world diseases into the Americas had a devastating impact on the new world population. In a matter of a few decades the environment in the new world changed radically. Native Americans suddenly became genetically unfit to live on the same ground that they had been successfully inhabiting for millennia.

In all these environments, status became a more important genetic competence when agriculture was introduced. In some geographical areas such as the new world, agriculture was introduced at a later date. However in all major populations, hierarchy became more important and pronounced once it was. As such, abilities to climb hierarchies became more selected for and evolution was accelerated. In each geographic area, genetic differentiation was accelerated, though it is likely that evolution most often found alternate routes to achieve the same traits. It is likely that in some other cases, existing gene structures held in common were selected for and advanced over time in different geographical areas.

Humans find it both emotionally and politically distasteful to associate success at status seeking as a positive genetic trait. It is especially disturbing to hear someone say that having these traits makes someone more genetically fit. Emotionally, the traits that make a person better at climbing hierarchies seem distasteful to many. The traits seem to be related to insincere flattery and betrayal. Politically, since most people are in the lower parts of a hierarchy, it is more palatable to attribute success to luck or hard work. Attributing success to survival fitness and genetic selection is thus uncomfortable in today's political environment. Though, of course, the genes you are born with and how your parents got them in the first place are a matter of luck. Chance is, after all, the fundamental mechanism of evolution.

Genes are also impacted by random variations not influenced by environmental selection. This process is referred to as genetic drift. Genetic drift can have a significant impact on smaller populations. The current theory is that a small group or small groups of modern humans left Africa roughly 50,000 years ago. After that, there would be different environmental impacts selecting for changes in this population, but the impact of genetic drift could also have been significant. Genetic drift would have been a strong force in these humans for generations until the population size of this group or these groups increased.

Given the current theories of the origin of mankind, genetic differences between West Asians and Europeans would be less than those between them and East Asians. The Australian and Native American populations would differ further still. One interesting projection is that while it is true that sub-Saharan African populations would be the most different from these other groups, inter-differences between different sub-Saharan African groups would be even greater than differences between sub-Saharan Africans overall and East Asians, Native Americans and Europeans.

Predicting the Coming Evolutionary Changes

On the evolutionary scale, the human race is changing very rapidly. Changing rapidly means that in multiple generations after hundreds of years that we will be modestly different.

One genetic trait that would be strongly selected for in today's environment, if it could be, is an emotional desire for children. This trait would be difficult to separate between cultural factors and genetic ones, but if there is currently a significant portion of the world population with a genetic predisposition to desiring children more than other people, this group could be strongly selected for and emerge and grow by a multiple of up to 2 over just a couple of generations. In a population like Japan's, with very low fertility, a group with a strong desire for children might get close to that adjustment in a single generation.

Another trait that is less adaptive in the current environment is a desire for status. Over time, this trait is likely to still be a positive selection factor, though much less so. This trait is likely to remain, but it will slowly decay over generations.

Those subcultures that isolate themselves from the wider world effectively, such as the Amish and Orthodox Jews, will continue to grow relative to the population as a whole for as long as they are able to maintain their separation. The ability to have and maintain faith may be a genetic quality and to that extent it will be a future selection criteria.

Over a long time, given a stable environment, genetic traits such as these would continue to grow and then radically alter the fertility profile of the world population. However, this process is likely to take many generations. The fertility crash would hit bottom and then over generations begin to rebound. The assumption of a stable environment is a huge hurdle, however. It is quite possible that the human environment will change even more radically in the future than it has up until now.

Given that it is unlikely that there will be a stable environment, at least in the near future, traits in today's world may make one adaptation genetically fit, but in a rapidly changing environment, it is likely many of those traits will lose their genetic benefit in little more than a generation.

In these descriptions, emphasis has been placed upon status seeking as an important aspect of human behavior and genetic competence. This is because status is important, but it is also a way to simplify the discussion. Human emotions are complicated and adaptive. Raw ambition will often not be the best evolutionary strategy. In complex interactions there is room for generosity, brotherhood and self-sacrifice. All of these can promote genetic competence and in mankind's rapidly changing society their application have all likely become subject to strong evolutionary pressure.

EVOLUTIONARY EMOTIONS AND WHAT THEY CAN CAUSE

Evolutionary psychology or the analysis of psychology based upon evolutionary pressures and priorities has faced criticism for post hoc analysis. In fact, the methodology can be a very useful tool. The discussion below provides some predictions based upon an evolutionary analysis of human psychology. It also turns out, that several longstanding economic conundrums can be explained through an evolutionary emotional analysis.

Shame, examined through the lens of evolution, must be a trait that supports survival. Human survival depends upon the cooperative action of human groups. However, since people are basically selfish, there must be some contract to ensure the necessary levels of reciprocity so that the cooperation doesn't breakdown. Shame is one of the emotions that cement reciprocal relationships.

Traditional economic theory posits that every economic actor, every human, maximizes their expected wealth within risk constraints. If this really were true, there would be no gambling and no lotteries. Economists sidestep the inconvenient existence of gambling and lotteries by assuming that they are a form of spending for entertainment or that the participants are ignorant of the true nature of the investment. The same situation exists with financial bubbles. Economists rely on the concept of an efficient market, or at least one that is mostly efficient. However, assets going through a financial bubble experience large gyrations during short periods without any similar changes in the fundamental nature of the asset.

Economists often blame this on the ignorance of a large herd.

Research has shown that economists' prediction of ignorant lottery players and lemming like investors isn't accurate. Participants of lotteries have been shown to be well aware of the risks involved and have been shown to, usually, wisely invest lottery proceeds. Similarly those investing in financial bubbles often are very aware of what they are doing and the risks involved. Economists are simply wrong about what peoples' goals really are.

Guilt and Shame

Human society thrives by close cooperation of individuals. Cooperation requires reciprocity. If a neighbor does someone a favor, cooperation requires that the person extending the favor have a strong expectation that the favor will be returned. There must be checks and balances to ensure that, within limited bounds, every individual contributes their share. Among the checks and balances are guilt and shame. Shame gives others some assurance that if an individual provides a favor to their neighbor, the neighbor will be inclined to return the favor sometime in the future.

Shame can also be driven by status seeking behavior. If an individual commits an act they feel guilty about, they will have a higher propensity to attempt to hide that act. If the act will be detrimental to the person's status, shame also provides the double advantage of reducing the likelihood that the action is repeated.

It has been shown, that when shame and guilt are more acute, the more likely an individual is to be exposed and suffer consequences. This has an impact on the attitudes and mores of society. For example, in the early Victorian era, in middle class and elite society, there were very limited social circles. Transportation was basic and most people interacted with neighbors of their own class. In such a society, a scandal was devastating to a family's social standing. Such a thing could severely curtail status and damage the parent's business opportunities or their children's prospects for a good match and a promising future. Consequently, society as a whole was very careful about appearances.

Contrast this to modern society. In the modern era, you can reinvent yourself. Especially in urban settings, there is always a new job, new friends and not infrequently a new family. In modern society, the consequences of scandal are minor and guilt and shame have a much-lessened impact. The change from Victorian to modern sensibilities didn't happen immediately, guilt and shame did not lessen overnight. It took more than a generation or two for shame to lessen after the society that spawned it had disappeared.

The Internet and social media have changed the world again. Acts that bring shame are captured permanently. People are being made examples of for small indiscretions and offhand comments they make. At first, people will begin to be more careful, but ultimately, in a generation or at most two, shame will return. People will begin to be much more discreet and they will begin to hide their dirty laundry.

Gambling, Lotteries and Other Financial Conundrums

Reuven Brenner et al, in their book, **A World of Chance: Betting on Religion, Games, Wall Street,** present interesting research on gambling, lotteries and financial bubbles.

Economists typically present gambling as either an entertainment or as an activity of unsophisticated or ignorant people. Brenner et al, provide evidence that this isn't true and that, in particular, participants in lotteries have a specific profile that casts doubt on the standard economists' view. Lottery players appear to be people who have reached a point in their lives where they have little opportunity to improve their status. The research shows as well that, in the main, lottery winners use the results of their winnings wisely.

Similarly, financial bubbles are difficult to reconcile with economists' models of efficient or even almost efficient markets. It is difficult to explain why assets can be worth such widely disparate amounts as they jump up and then crash down a short time later and still say the market was rational.

Lotteries

Economists view people as risk adverse actors that will put their own funds at risk only if their expected return is greater than even. A risk adverse actor would not bet on the flip of a coin unless they got more if they won than they'd lose when they lost. According to standard economic theory then, gambling could only happen if people were gambling for entertainment or were fools unable to correctly estimate the risks they are taking. According to the economist, lotteries would only be popular to people with limited understanding, because the expected gain is about half the money wagered

However a biologist would view their behavior differently. In the human evolutionary environment, having status meant non-linear opportunities for mating and increasing offspring in the long-term. In the simplified model, this translated into humans, especially males that were seeking to gain status and fighting not to lose it. Males in the bottom half of hierarchies could look forward to minimal opportunities for progeny and those limited opportunities extended to their children and near relations. In that group, a high level of risk taken to improve status, and improve the status of their progeny, would be genetically advantageous. According to the biologist, lotteries make sense because the added progeny, now and in future generations, is exponentially greater than the progeny, if any, lost. At least that would have been true in the *evolutionary environment*. In today's world, the windfall would lead to greatly increased status, but likely lead to a much lower future long term expected level of offspring

Surveys of the people that buy lottery tickets reinforce the biologists' position. The typical participant is someone who is past his youth and in or beyond middle age. The person will likely be employed in a steady position, but have little opportunity for greater advancement. To such a person, losing a few dollars in the lottery would have zero impact on his current status. Playing and winning the lottery, however, would allow them to leapfrog, as Brenner et al puts it, into a status level several rungs above their current position.

The use of funds by the winners also reinforces the view that lottery participants are not unsophisticated fools. The typical winner makes modest adjustments to their lifestyle, helps children and grandchildren with their education and makes sound conservative investments. The popular image of a winner as a spendthrift that buys luxury cars, gambles and fritters the winnings away undoubtedly exists, but they are the exception, not the rule.

Lotteries and gambling in general are phenomena that cannot be explained in the standard economic theories of human financial behavior. To accommodate the behavior economists are forced to either label the behavior as entertainment or label the participants as ignorant or unsophisticated. Lotteries in particular can be explained biologically however. Winning a lottery successfully increases status. Playing the lottery is not a sound strategy to increase wealth, but for some people it is a successful strategy to improve long-term progeny. That is if humans were still in their *evolutionary environment*. In this case, examining human behavior using an evolutionary emotional lens provides an explanation for a longstanding economic conundrum.

Financial Bubbles

Financial bubbles are cases where a category of asset is traded, often in a frenzied way. The asset quickly increases in price to a large amount and then collapses back down to a much-reduced amount. Examples of financial bubbles include the real estate bubble culminating in the 2007-2008 crash. The 'Dot-Com' high tech stock bubble ending in early 2000 and the Japanese asset bubble that decayed over the decade of the 1990's.

Economists generally ascribe to the efficient market theory. According to this theory, assets will be correctly priced since there are a sufficient number of knowledgeable investors that will have strong financial incentives to trade in mispriced assets and that will ultimately correct any mispricing to within the cost of trading. Economists often acknowledge exceptions, such as bubbles, which are unexplained phenomena where the markets are inefficient.

In a financial bubble virtually all the participants do well during the upward phase. In the early stages of the bubble's increase, few individuals will know other participants in the market. As the assets continue their upward run participation increases. More people buy into the bubble and more direct contact with bubble participants becomes likely. Toward the later stages it becomes very likely that there are many people, in offices, neighborhoods or social groups that are participating and experiencing strong asset appreciation.

From a financial point of view, it will look as if traditional valuation models indicate that investing in the asset is foolish. For real estate, the price of the property will be well below the building costs or the ratio of the price to rents will be low. For a stock, the price to earnings ratio will be oversized and new, alternate pricing models will be floated. Those people that haven't participated to this point have every reason they had previously not to jump in, but many will anyway. They do this for biological reasons rather than financial ones.

Entering the market at this point is a hedge against losing status relative to peers. The peers in this case might be neighbors, co-workers or friends. There will certainly be stories of early participants with returns that have made them relatively rich. If a person's peers continue on the current path, they might achieve the same status level of these others. A group of peers breaking out of your status group to a level beyond would have been a significant genetic threat to someone in the *evolutionary environment*. This is because their mating opportunities, now and in future generations would eclipse those that didn't break out.

Of course it is not the case in our modern world. The increase in wealth and status might lead to marginally better opportunities for increased progeny, but it certainly wouldn't lead to exponentially improved opportunities. The emotional drivers are still within us however. People are smart enough to recognize that the investment is a poor one. They are performing a different calculation. They are acting on emotion in a way designed long ago and unbeknownst to them to protect their and their children's chances to pass on their genes into the future generations.

Here again, an evolutionary, biological explanation of emotions explains a long standing unexplained phenomena of human behavior from economics. People are investing in an asset they know is overpriced. It is an emotional decision made despite that knowledge. However the fear of losing status compared to your immediate peers is great enough to drive many to take the plunge and invest. The investment is in fact a rational hedge against legitimate fears of losing status and it would have been a wise biological bet, if the person truly understood why they were doing it and if we were still in the *evolutionary environment*.

Investing in a Bubble, an Aside

The above analysis reveals what someone's strategy should be for investing in an asset bubble. Since the asset typically goes through a pattern of rising quickly and then crashing, the opportune time to sell is just before the asset crashes. Selling anytime on the upward trajectory would still leave the investor with positive returns and since there are multiple upward price movements of assets that aren't bubbles there are no sure signs of the asset peak. There is one solid sign, however, that an asset should definitely be exited. If the investor has multiple acquaintances and associates that are not typically active investors who are talking about or purchasing the asset, it is time to exit the market. This is both a sure sign that it is a financial bubble and a sure sign that the bubble is near its peak. Since asset crashes are generally long tailed, the exit should be final. Any return to the market for that asset should be in years, not months.

Genocide

After World War II, there were many proclamations about the evils of the Axis powers. The world looked upon the horrors of concentration camps with revulsion. In the aftermath, the common cry was *never again*. Enough time and history has past to recognize that as a forlorn hope.

Genocide is the ultimate genetic victory. Wiping out the opposing tribe and inheriting their territory. Over the human experience it has happened again and again. Work up hate to get over inhibitions, then dehumanize. This behavior is not gone. The world will face this again and again in the future.

In some cases, genocide is born out of hate, usually inspired by historical events that often have nothing to do with the current populations. In other cases, genocide is inspired by fear. If the enmity between groups is bitter and long standing, given the nature of humans, the fear may be entirely justified. The collapsing fertility of some groups may trigger desperate measures born out a fear, most likely an irrational fear for survival.

This type of fear may have helped fuel the Russian and Ukrainian crisis, and may be driving Iranian behavior. It may create behaviors in Europe toward Muslim immigrant populations in the long run that appear unthinkable today.

Many West Asian immigrants to European countries and Britain have formed separate, insulated societies. They show hostility and often contempt toward their host countries, and have high rates of unemployment and crime. They are also increasing due to further immigration and higher fertility compared to the declining host population.

Many have suggested that the result of the continued immigration and disparate fertility will be the islamization of Europe. This is highly unlikely. In the first place, fertility of the Islamic population in Europe has been declining and will continue to decline significantly. Also, these populations are currently small, usually in the 5% range and at most near 10% of the host population.

However, if there is no trend toward assimilation, there will ultimately be harsh measures taken against these isolated Islamic communities. The longer this takes to implement, the harsher the measures will be. These measures will not ultimately be due to prejudice against the immigrants. They will ultimately be due to irrational fears for survival. Escalation of the Shia-Sunni conflict in the Middle East along with the nuclearization of Iran and Saudi Arabia will exacerbate the problems.

Evolutionary psychology predicts that in many ways humans are craven animals. Their efforts are primarily directed toward their own and their offspring's status and they tailor their emotions to best achieve this. Humans will naturally create emotions of love and friendship as a way to gain commitment from other humans in this quest. They will cooperate, if by cooperating they gain themselves. They will feel shame, but only in proportion to their likelihood of being caught. They will work as a group to develop hatred for an out-group and dehumanize them and, if the opportunity arises, slaughter them either opportunistically or in fear, acting first against the out-group before it can be done to them. This nature is unattractive, but can be used to explain and predict human behaviors in a broad sense.

Dennis Marx

ECONOMY & CULTURE

Economy

An Economy of Old People

As people age, they typically increase savings and investments and hold less debt. Simultaneously, their tolerance for risk diminishes. In this environment return on investment will drop, especially for low risk investments. Relative to the risk free return, high-risk investments will receive a greater premium, though it is likely the return on capital overall will be limited.

Much has been said elsewhere about the strain on retirement systems and the focus on senior focused business. These issues will be more pronounced as time progresses and will exist even more worldwide than in the US.

Retirement ages will increase. Some of this will be unofficial as low returns on retirement portfolios increase pressure on seniors to find other sources of income. Some will be state mandated as public finances come under increasing pressure.

There will be hundreds of small changes in products, advertising and entertainment. There will be strains and necessary compromises in health care. Many countries, with government funded health services, will introduce restrictions on end of life decisions and develop a focus on palliative care.

Falling Population

A flip side of the aging of the population is the falling population and a new scarcity of young people. As the overall population ages, the dearth of young people will grow, slowly creeping up through schools and then into the workforce. In this environment, real property will become less valuable.

Childless couples will grow to greater share of all couples. It is possible that as many as 25% of couples will never have children. The current childless rate for women in their late forties in Italy is 24%. These will be people with significant disposable income. It is likely these families begin to be recognized as a target-marketing niche. The marketing may focus on off-season travel, urban living and smaller, luxurious housing. When smaller families and childless couples predominate; inheritances are likely to become larger.

In Europe, currently 50% of families only have one child. In many cases, this is a transitional phenomena and a second child will be forthcoming. On the other hand, in many cases they will not. A rough estimate, based primarily on early results from Europe, is that by the end of the century the human race will be made up of 20% childless and 40% single child families.

Economic Growth

Typically, economic growth has two components. The first is the increased per capita income and the second is the extra income due to increased population. In the future, GDP increases will become a per capita GDP increase and a reduction due to populations falling. The overall economies of the world will grow much less.

Malthusian Economy

A Malthusian economy is one where population growth outstrips resources. When that happened, the vast majority of the population lived at subsistence levels. This is dire poverty with families forced into a lifestyle that would make the very poorest of the poor in the United States appear rich. Throughout history, up until roughly 1820, the world was usually in a Malthusian state. There are many who are currently arguing that a Malthusian state is inevitable, with the implication that strong population controls are required in order to stave off a coming disaster.

The Malthus economy requires a population growing faster that resource availability is increasing. We are currently far from such a state. GDP per capita, in every corner of the globe, is well above subsistence levels and in almost every region is improving. This is a measure of how resource availability is increasing above and beyond population increases.

The current and spreading fertility collapse is also delaying any day of reckoning. Meanwhile, technology improvements that will expand available resources are accumulating and coming online at what appears to be an increasing rate, greatly improving productivity. Humans may yet reach an end to the current prosperity boom and fall back into a Malthusian world, but the reckoning is centuries or more away, not decades.

Thomas Malthus

Thomas Malthus was an English philosopher who wrote an influential essay on populations at the end of the 18th century. The fundamental point was that populations grow exponentially until they reach a bare subsistence level. He emphasized that any technological improvement would reduce the overall poverty for a short period, but that the population would rise until resource availability forced the population back into a bare subsistence level standard of living. Essentially, the population would grow until death from malnutrition, disease and starvation limited further population growth.

This was the result of the Agrarian revolution, even more people living in absolute poverty than before agriculture and a small elite living well. It has been argued that life in early agrarian societies was worse than the lives of hunter gather societies. It has even been argued that it was poor choice to live that way. It was not a choice. Agrarian societies could live more densely on the land. Their genes were the ones placed into the next generation. Their genes were the successful ones. The choice was made by the necessities of survival.

Within a generation after Malthus wrote the essay, modern industrial nations began a period where both populations and prosperity increased simultaneously due to a continuing flow of technological improvements. This period has lasted until the present day and has expanded beyond industrial nations to the entire world. What has happened to the Malthusian theory is that the rate of technological improvements have outstripped population growth for the last 200 years creating a unique period of prosperity in human existence.

Today, the Malthusian economic model in various forms is the basis of numerous political movements. The push for population control uses many of his arguments. It is also closely related to environmentalist movements.

Sustaining Prosperity

The key to continuously improving prosperity is to continue to innovate, to engineer these innovations into the economy and have the benefits spread throughout the economy. With only 200 years of history, the assumption that innovation will continue forever is highly suspect. However, it is likely that it will be sustainable for the foreseeable future based upon the current innovation pipeline.

There are a great many improvements that already exist and are currently being implemented through the world's economies. There are many more that experience has shown are easily doable and just require engineering implementation. Finally, there are an even greater number where current knowledge shows what may be possible with further effort.

Growth Through Innovation

For 200 years, technological improvements have driven a 2% annual growth in per capita GDP in the industrialized world. These increases have lately been spreading across the globe. They came later and they have had starts and stops, but they have expanded and are now built into everyone's expectations.

This was not always the case. For thousands of years almost everyone on the globe lived at a subsistence level. During that period there were innovations, however after the innovation occurred, the population density increased leaving more people, at a greater density, living at a subsistence level. The innovations happened at too slow a pace to outstrip population growth. Beginning 200 years ago, the innovations improved farming, transportation and manufacturing at a rate greater than population growth, enough to improve per capita GDP by 2% each year. Since then, technology has continued to outstrip population growth at roughly the same rate.

This will continue for the foreseeable future, because there is a significant backlog of technological improvements that haven't worked their way into the economy. First, there are a significant number of technological improvements already developed and working that have been implemented in some businesses, but have yet to be implemented broadly. There are also significant advancements requiring modest engineering development to begin to make useful. Finally, there are many possible innovations on the horizon each of which could potentially have large positive impact on productivity.

Existing Technologies

This will not be a survey on up and coming technologies, but merely point to some examples in each of these cases. One obvious case of an existing technology that is being implemented across business and improving productivity is electronic billing and payments. Electronic business to customer billing and payment is still fairly early in its adoption cycle, but business to business adoption is further along. Business to business invoices used to be delivered as paper and companies stored their invoices in files. Later the invoices were delivered as images and stored electronically. Now more companies are requesting electronic delivery and developing standardized formats. These are gradually replacing expensive and less accurate manual data entry processes.

There are many other, similarly familiar, technologies advancing through economies and improving business productivity. Many people have seen these develop and advance over their lifetimes until, by now, the concepts have become second nature. As more producers and consumers adopt these and as more interface standards are developed, industry-by-industry, it becomes just another standard business practice.

This is, of course, only one of many improvements being implemented across business that improve productivity. These arrays of now simple things that were once hard to imagine are now driving per capita GDP growth across the world.

Known Technology Being Developed

One controversial innovation based upon known technology is self-driving cars. On average, Americans currently drive over one hour each day. Self-driving cars have the potential to free up significant time to millions of people and greatly improve safety.

Popular culture usually focuses on the energy and pollution issues in regards to difficult commutes and auto travel. The greatest loss, however, is the loss of peoples' time. It is true that many, if not most, people will use the free time for leisure activities, or may even prefer driving, but many other people will use the time for work. They will program, study, plan or write, answer the morning's emails and attend conference calls. Without the requirement of a driver, it might become economically feasible for a service to have cars, installed with a 'car' office pick up 3 or 4 people and provide door-to-door service on a daily basis.

This is one of a million possible small steps from current technology. Most of these won't become possible or will be superseded. Many, however, will have an impact and they will continue to drive productivity improvements

Unproven Technology Currently Being Worked On

This is a wildly mixed bag from nanotechnology to fusion reactors and reusable space launchers that reduce the costs of reaching space. Each of these could greatly improve human productivity. Some will ultimately turn out feasible and some won't. The ones that do will impact all our lives.

This discussion of implementation of technology is not an attempt to predict the future technologies that will be entering our lives, but was to argue that, at least for the foreseeable future, innovation will be driving human productivity upward in the same way it has for the last 200 years. In many ways the development of new technologies seems to have accelerated and that there exists a large backlog of innovations waiting to be implemented into our daily lives.

Technological Innovation

Given the pipeline of technological innovation it is very unlikely that the modern historical pattern of prosperity will decline in the next 100 years. Unless governments act to restrain technology, technological innovation is likely to accelerate.

Population

The recent fertility collapse is not something envisioned by Malthus. The fact that many of the political movements inspired by his vision wish to ignore, minimize or deny the collapse highlights the difficulties that the collapse has to the Malthusian model.

If the *evolutionary environment* remains stable over time, the fertility collapse will reverse itself. Given the strong selective nature of the collapse, it might reverse materially in only a few generations. At that point, if continued changes in the human environment don't continue to suppress fertility, and if innovation is curtailed by a reduction in human inventiveness or government intervention, and if humans don't find an increase in their environment in near space, then Malthusian concerns may again be valid.

Until then, those groups invoking these concerns are, in reality, merely attempting to gain control over other humans, which is a very human trait. They are attempting to gain power and status. By attempting to improve their status by controlling other people and limiting these others opportunities for progeny, they are simply following their base emotional programming. Of course in today's environment, it won't provide the survival advantage it was designed to do. Yet they are driven to try to accomplish dominance unaware that they just puppets moved by emotional strings that they don't understand in order to accomplish goals that in modern times have lost their purpose.

World Economy

World Media fixates on inequality and on countries, like China, that break out of their recent historical mode. There has been a revolution occurring, however, that has had very little press or attention. The poor, worldwide, are becoming richer. This has happened in a material sense and GDP per capita numbers have been showing it. The per capita growth rate in most non-industrial countries has been steady and positive and it will continue that way. Simultaneously, the costs of technological innovations have undergone a long, steady decline. Cell phones are within reach of the masses, not just of industrial countries, but of the world. The same is true for computers and Internet access.

The modern world is quickly invading every nook and cranny where humans live and this process will continue. People today that lived with what average Americans had 50 years ago, in the mid-sixties, would be considered poor today. In 35 years, poverty will again be redefined to a much higher standard of living.

Culture

The aging population will also impact world culture. In many ways the aging population will cause cultural change to occur more slowly, leading to an *ossified society*. For the first time in human history the population pyramid will be inverted. The older generations will overshadow the younger. Each new generation will be hidden, invisible.

Other trends are likely. With the population of younger males dropping, crime will fall. Childless adults, childless couples and single child families will become cultural phenomena. With falling prices, and rising worldwide wealth, connectivity will broaden and deepen and spread to everyone alive. This and new technology may greatly impact fertility by interfering in male sexuality. This access may also, as every blemish and fault becomes immortalized in bits and bytes, create a new Victorian era as shame makes a comeback. The new Victorian era will have a different set of mores than the previous one, but it will still be straight-laced and judgmental.

Culture of an Aging Society

In every region of the world, the number and percentage of older people is growing to unprecedented levels. This growth is driven by greatly reduced mortality at older ages combined with collapsing fertility worldwide.

The world's over 50 population will nearly double, from slightly over 1.6 billion today to 3.2 billion in 2050. The percentage of the population over 50 will increase from 22% in 2015 to over 1/3rd in 2050. Through the rest of 21st century, this process will accelerate.

In Asia and Latin America the population over 50 will more than double from 2015 to 2050, while the population under 50 will drop. In Africa, the population over 50 will rise 323%, while the under 50 population is projected to increase only 80%. The over 50 crowd will increase more slowly in industrialized regions and be limited to 25%, but that is only because the population there is already older. The aging of the world will result in, not only great economic changes, but significant cultural changes as well.

A Culture of Old People

With an older population it is likely that there will be an increased resistance to change. This will occur in entertainment, education, products, advertising, societal organization and lifestyle. There will be fewer opportunities for advancement. This will effect everyone, but since the young often begin their lives closer to the bottom, it will have an outsized impact on them. There could also be significant increases in efforts to suppress disruptive innovations.

As a generation ages much of their tastes remain constant. The tastes include music, actors, television shows and movies among a wide array of other things. It will include media preferences, as new mediums of communication emerge, as well as how they access their options. The people that are famous to a generation stay famous in that generation and the musicians, actors and personalities they are attracted to remain stable. It was hard to find a radio station in the 1990's focused on music of the 40's and 50's, but the music of the baby boom generation, the music of the 60's and 70's, is still widely played to this day. When the peak of the population becomes older, their preferences will endure much longer.

By the time people turn 50, they have strong brand awareness and loyalty. They tend to buy the same products from the same manufacturers. Because of that, companies are willing to spend heavily on advertising to younger groups in order to establish brand awareness and gain brand loyalty. This advertising becomes a good, long-term, investment. Entertainment choices are built around this paradigm. Media companies today create programming, choose actors and spokespeople, and pick venues with building brand loyalty in younger people in mind. If the population of younger people to attract becomes smaller and smaller, then the return on these advertising dollars decreases and building brand awareness and loyalty becomes a more questionable investment. All the decisions about programming, actors and venues will be questioned as well, further reducing the new generation's impact on society and culture.

Most society is organized through hierarchies. In some cultures the organizations are primarily governmental and bureaucratic. Some have tribal hierarchies. The freer, modern industrial societies tend to have a broader range of hierarchical types. They still have government and affiliated bureaucracies, but will also have a wide array of non-government ones associated with business, charitable, religious and union organizations, and multiple political parties among others.

In each one of these hierarchies, even if they have been successful, there are a very limited number of top spots to be filled. The people in those top positions will have a tendency to remain there and with a shrinking population, these hierarchies will be less likely to grow. Society will become less dynamic. Organizations will have less new blood and more people will be stuck in lower level positions.

One option for younger, innovative people is to start other, competing organizations. With fewer young people, these are, unfortunately, likely to be less numerous. It is also likely, that older groups, being resistant to change, organize to attempt to limit disruptive innovations and make these start-ups even fewer still.

The Ossified Society

One thing to understand is that all people will be affected by the tendency of hierarchies to stagnate. Over time, promotions, whether they are in business, government bureaucracies, or other organizations, will be harder and harder to obtain. Younger people will be the most directly affected, because they will have started after the freeze began, but everyone not already at the top will be impacted. As organizations cease to grow, upward mobility will become more difficult. This situation is liable to accelerate through the 21st century and at least through the 1st half of the 22nd.

The Invisible Generations

Each generation's artists, innovators, and leaders take time to establish themselves. As population cohorts become smaller and smaller, it will become more difficult to be noticed and it will be harder to have an impact on society, culture, business or politics. As the younger populations become smaller, they will have more difficulty coalescing on cultural icons and trends. They will, therefore, be more splintered. Movements will become difficult to form. Each passing generation will become more easily absorbed into the older society in which they live and more difficult to differentiate.

Other Predictions

The drop in fertility and the future population profile will also result in a couple miscellaneous changes. Crime will drop. There will be a growing number of childless adults and couples as well as a growing percentage of single child families.

Crime Will Fall

Young males commit the vast majority of crime. An 18-year-old male is 3 times as likely to commit a crime as an 18-year-old female. They are twice as likely to commit a crime as a 24-year-old male, 3 times as likely as a male in their early thirties and 12 times as likely to commit a crime as a male in their 50s. As the average age of the population increases, crime will decline. Since the population of young men is set to take a steep decline, there will be a steep decline in crime as well.

Childless Adults Will Become Common and Infertility Will Increase

In traditional societies, where women marry young and use no contraceptives, less than 3% of women go childless. In modern society, the numbers are much higher. Some women choose not to have children. Many women choose to delay starting families and that greatly increases their chances of infertility.

As of 2009 only 3% of women in India in their late 40's had gone childless. This is close to the number predicted to be infertile. In Japan 13% of women in their late 40's were childless. In the US, it was 17% and in Italy it was 24%. These women started their childbearing years 35 years ago, in the early 80's. During this period, the fertility collapse was in its early stages in the industrialized world, and non-existent in developing nations. The numbers in Japan, the US and Italy are likely predictive of the childless women to be expected in many developing nations in 2050.

Many of these women will remain childless voluntarily. However, as more and more women go to college and receive higher levels of education, as more of them choose careers, or otherwise delay childbearing, infertility will also be a factor. Typically, women in their early 20's have low infertility rates, well below 5%. As women age, however, infertility rises. Women in their early 30's have infertility rates in the 10% range. This rises to over 15% in their late 30's and over 30% in their early 40's. As women choose education, careers and lifestyle over childrearing, there will be more and more childless women entering their late 40's.

Single Child Families

Currently, about 50% of Europe's families with children have an only child, 34% have 2 and about 16% have 3 or more. As low fertility settles across the world, a similar distribution will become normal. The view from the adults' point of view will be a world with few children. From the childrens' perspective however, 75% of children will still have one or more siblings.

A couple of very unique situations are about to occur. We are about to enter a world where a significant portion of women above 50, 15% to as many as 25%, will have no direct connection to the next generation. Of the remaining adults, half of the women and almost half of parents in general, will have had only 1 child. All their eggs, genetically speaking, will have been put in a single basket. There may have been times in the past, where infant and childhood mortality created a similar result, but never a situation where the profile occurred by choice.

The impact on the culture where so many have no experience of children will be profound. In many ways, there will be obvious aspects. Less tolerance of children misbehaving in public, for instance. In other ways, the impacts are likely to be subtle, however, and difficult to see.

Similarly, the impacts on a society where so many parents only have a single child will be varied. Much has been written on how an only child is different. Very little consideration has been expended on how the parents of single children will differ in outlook and behavior, and they will outnumber their children 2 to 1.

Reproduction

While inequality will continue, poverty in an absolute sense will continue to diminish. Most of the poorer countries have been experiencing per capita GDP growth. War and other social upheavals account for most of negative economic growth seen. Almost the entire world is rising up from poverty and as they do, they are becoming connected to the modern world. They are getting more education, using cell phones, and connecting to the Internet.

Over time, the absolute levels of poverty will continue to drop and at the same time connectivity to the wide world will get less expensive and become more ubiquitous. All this will become more and more disruptive to traditional modes of life and it will drive fertility down. In all likelihood, it will reduce fertility farther and faster in the countries that are currently the poorest to a greater extent than anyone expects.

Sex and Fertility

Meanwhile, human nature combined with science will be interfering with the male sex drive to an even greater extent in the future. There is always someone that will turn new technologies toward pornography and sexual gratification, and because of the power of the sexual drive in men; there will always be a legion of men that will be lured into it.

Pornography flourishes on the Internet. Males flock to it. Including many that would never have had easy access. Some of the greatest use of Internet porn occurs in sexually restrictive societies such as in the Middle East.

When new technologies emerge that can be used to satisfy the human male sexual drive, they will be used to satisfy the male sexual drive. The end result is that pornography and sex tools will become ever more realistic and even more accessible.

Two upcoming technologies that fit this description are virtual reality and robotics. Virtual reality currently is primarily focused on a obtaining a realistic visual and audio world, but ultimately will incorporate tactile sensations. Human like robots are most likely further out, mainly due to the costs involved, but they will be developed. It may be done in fits and starts, but robotic capabilities are growing rapidly. In both cases, at every intermediate step that the technologies go through, there will be applications developed and used to satisfy the male sex drive.

The impact on fertility could be dramatic. The experience these technologies provide could become sufficient to derail many males from attempting to secure mates. Males, already obsessed with computer gaming, may become even more so. The male interest in, and behavior and attitude toward women might derail the application of their sex drive and have a strong impact on fertility. The overall cultural impact could be even greater.

The Internet As the New Small Town

Guilt and shame increase when a person believes they will be caught in a base act and increases more if a person believes there will be consequences. The Victorian age was built on the guilt that came from small, familiar circles of society. In those societies, there was no getting away from a scandal. All of your friends and family and all of your acquaintances would find out and then, all of your and your family's prospects for improved status would be in jeopardy.

As the world urbanized and mobility increased, family ties were lessoned. Circles of society became more fluid. People had greater and greater opportunities to reinvent themselves. Shame was lessened, because the likelihood of consequences was reduced. Guilt became less acute when it became less likely that far-flung families and friends would discover the cause of the guilt or feel the consequences. Over a few generations, parents focused less on the dangers of scandal. As a result, guilt and shame were lessened. Things that were scandalous before started to became acceptable.

With the introduction of the Internet and social media, once again it is becoming hard to hide from base actions. In the new Internet age there are sometimes dire consequences.

A woman was virtually pilloried after she made an offhand tweet. The tweet wasn't meant to be offensive and in fact wasn't, but it was taken as offensive. Her acquaintances shunned her and friends stepped back. She lost her job and had trouble finding another. She was branded, maybe not with an A, for Adultery, but with an R for Racist.

A man contributed money to a cause. At the time of the contribution, most people thought it a popular cause. Years later, many people that supported his position at the time turned on him and condemned him. He lost his high status job. Suddenly, the world has entered the beginnings of a new Victorian age.

It will take awhile for the effects to set in. It might be a generation or two. The ingredients are all there now however. A few people will be broadly and publically humiliated. More will be humiliated in their local circles, but they will realize that the scandal will follow them, immortalized in cyberspace.

Everyone will see this happen to someone and they will be more careful. Parents will tell their children to be more careful, because there are now consequences. People will see the consequences that family, friends and co-workers are put through. When a person applies for a job, the employer will search the Internet and based upon what they find, they will quietly be passed over. Enough people will feel the inner workings and the message will spread.

Of course it won't be exactly the Victorian age. It will be a different and varying set of values placed on people. If in the Victorian age, you were shunned for homosexuality, today it will be for contributing to a wrong cause and later it may be for shunning the person who contributed to the wrong cause. Nevertheless, moral codes will become more strictly enforced.

The crux of the new Victorian era is that the world will be able to uncover something bad that was done when someone was 12, or 20 or 40. It may have even been acceptable behavior at the time. Something that everyone thought was acceptable 10 years ago or 20 years ago may not be acceptable anymore, but the record will be out there and people will be condemned for it. Over time and experience, people will learn to be more and more careful. Parents will pass the experience on to their children. Shame and guilt will return in force.

How Will Today's Society Be Viewed in 100 Years?

One hundred years ago, the Victorian age was being destroyed in a great world war. Today, the Victorians are mocked for their hypocrisy. They are mocked for being judgmental, for being bigots and for being close-minded.

Of course all of that is unfair. The Victorians could provide color and explanation for everything they stood for. The criticism is based upon a simplified view and the new emphasis is based upon new information. It is natural to simplify, to misconstrue, to mock and condemn and so 100 years hence, it will happen again.

Highly Speculative Predictions

These are some highly speculative predictions about how the current culture will be viewed 100 years hence. This is primarily meant for its amusement value.

Sexual relations will become more private and hidden. The current period will be condemned for being reckless about the mental and physical health issues around sex. With the rise of wealth and power more broadly spread worldwide and especially in Asia, more traditional mores and a condemnation of sexual license will occur, including a backlash against non-standard sex acts, which will be condemned as a Western influence.

Western hypersensitivity about racial and other discriminations will be mocked as the work of hyper-moralistic hypocrites. The one sided and selective nature of all the outrage will be pointed out and mocked. Discrimination will be proclaimed as a natural feeling that when suppressed builds up in an unhealthy way.

Genetic data will be used to support the idea that races are different. Multiple groups, lead by the Chinese will openly state that they are the superior race and condemn the current period as unscientific and hypocritical. Race relations overall, however, will be much better, with much less emphasis on peoples differences.

The art of the period, mostly the visual arts, will be condemned as shallow and catering to puerile interests using highly simplified moral messaging. In the arts, the period will be considered a low point of development, based upon a decaying culture and will be compared unfavorably to the high western cultural period between 1550 and 1915.

INVESTING FOR THE 21ST CENTURY

Investments are not the primary topic of this book. However, an understanding of the future is a great asset for life and investment planning. One of the major, and obvious, results of an aging worldwide population is the increased downward pressure on the returns of all traditional assets, especially the more conservative ones. Another, less obvious and less sure prediction, is that real estate assets will depreciate relative to inflation. This will be more true for rural and suburban real estate. Urban real estate, in areas where crime is low and services are readily available could, on the other hand, do very well.

Labor worldwide will become more expensive. Therefore, industries that successfully implement automation or that provide automation services to old line industries can do very well. This will be especially true for automating and simplifying customer service.

With investment returns under pressure due to the competition for returns in passive investments, it might be best make non-traditional investments. These require a combination of low liquidity, smaller, fractured markets and specialized knowledge. They often require a steep learning curve, specialized skills, and a considerable investment of time. One category that might do well in the coming environment are concierge services targeted at seniors, childless couple or small families. These will need to be positioned in highly selected geographies.

Returns on Traditional Assets

With an aging population, a much higher percentage of the world population than ever before will have accumulated assets over a lifetime. This will create a high demand for investments. The demand will be especially high for low risk high quality investments, since much of the money will be directed toward secure retirement. This does not mean there will be an end to periods of high volatility. Economic panics, financial bubbles and catastrophic global events such as wars will still go on, but low total returns on stocks and abnormally high valuations, such as those that are being seen currently, will become more commonplace. Low real interest rates, the interest paid above inflation, will continue throughout the century. This will be especially true for government bonds.

Real Estate

Real estate, as an asset class will do poorly. Exceptions will exist in geographies conducive to seniors, people without children, or small families. These will primarily be urban settings with low crime, mild climates, and a high levels of services. Rural and suburban properties will languish. Smaller, luxurious dwellings in highly desirable locales will do well. Large houses, especially those in rural areas will do poorly.

Businesses

Labor in third world countries will begin to command a higher wage. This will accelerate the move to automation in services as well as in manufacturing. Those businesses that make self service simple, or that show other businesses how to make self service simple and convenient will do well. Anyone can recognize this when they use a service. If it worked well and satisfied them, the business could do well. This is true in customer service at the retail level and in business to business environments.

Concierge Services

Businesses providing concierge type services to seniors and parents with either no children or an only child will be a growth industry. For example fast food restaurants will have a difficult time surviving. There will be fewer children and large families to patronize them, and labor costs will increase. On the other hand, with more seniors and smaller or childless families, more upscale and quality specialty restaurants will be in demand. This is just an example of the type of change. Businesses providing expensive, personal services can do well if they can be readily accessed in urban areas if they provide convenience and service.

Investing in these business requires recognizing a service that appeals to seniors, childless couples or only child families and shows an understanding that they need to carefully target resources to these niches and in the geographies they inhabit. Entrepreneurs starting these businesses need to recognize the same dynamic.

Dennis Marx

FINAL NOTES

Human fertility has collapsed or is collapsing in every region and country of the globe. This is happening because humans are genetically unfit to survive in the modern world. Humans have been evolving at an accelerated rate, but the changes in the human environment have accelerated even faster and human evolution has not kept up.

The primary failure point has been the emotional computer that drove human behavior. It does not work in the modern world. Using a simplified view of human emotional drivers, satisfying the status seeking behaviors in humans and satisfying the male sex drive is no longer resulting in procreation. Meanwhile traditional societies across the world are entering into the modern world and their emotional computers are failing as they enter.

While inequality may be growing, on an absolute measure, bare subsistence poverty is disappearing. Almost every poor country in the world is experiencing steady per capita GDP growth. The exceptions are almost all due to war or other similar social upheavals. Some are growing faster than others, but in comparison to the world before 1800, it is unprecedented. As a result, every corner of the earth is becoming wired into the modern world and because of that fertility will fall faster in the developing world than any of the current predictions.

By the end of the 21st century, the world population will be declining steadily. Even before that the younger population will begin to decline, while the population of older people is still increasing. The result will be that further population declines are built into the demographics and that the percentage of the population that is older is very large and growing. The new age distribution of the world will be completely unprecedented and profoundly impact culture and economics.

Predictions on how the culture and the economy of the world will change are very speculative. Broadly, risk taking will be reduced. Economically, less risky investments will yield low returns and property values will decrease overall. Culturally, younger generations will have an increasingly difficult time finding a voice.

In this new environment, human evolution will accelerate. Given somewhat stable conditions, a new emotional computer will arrive that favors increased fertility and, at the same time is more resistant to the constant changes likely to occur in the human environment. These changes will be highly selected for in the new environment and they are likely to dominate the population in a much shorter time than would likely be predicted. It may occur in centuries and not millennia and may even be felt within the space of several generations.

AFTERWORD AND REFERENCES

References for *A Survey of Demographics*

These concepts are an integration of ideas from numerous sources.

The Survey of Demographics heavily used data from the US Census. The US Census's International Data Base contains data on past and current populations and projects these through to 2050:

http://www.census.gov/population/international/index.html,

Pew research has done a report on intermarriage rates between groups. According to the report 8.4% of all marriages are mixed race and 15% of new marriages are. The report shows a strong increase in intermarriage overall and high rates of intermarriage for Asians and Hispanics at 28% and 26% respectively.

http://www.pewsocialtrends.org/2012/02/16/the-rise-of-intermarriage/

An odd thing about the results is the low US Census numbers for people of mixed race. The US Census shows 2.4% of Americans of mixed race. A lower number than the intermarriage rate would be expected to indicate since the intermarriage rate is on the upswing and the population impact would lag. Though 2.4% seems quite low even then and is probably due to bias against mixed race built into the US Census methodology. For instance 8.4% of total marriages are mixed race, but only 4.1% of children are designated as mixed race. The number of children would lag much less than the overall population number. Currently, 15% of all new marriages are interracial, but the US Census predicts that only 8.9% of the children in 2060 will of mixed race. It seems likely that whatever the US Census is doing, it is counting only about half of mixed race children.

http://quickfacts.census.gov/qfd/states/00000.html

References for *Why Has Fertility Collapsed?*

A new paper on a strong y-Chromosome bottleneck occurring at the dawn of the Agrarian age is shining some very interesting light on evolutionary pressures that began emerging in the Neolithic era:

http://www.ncbi.nlm.nih.gov/pubmed/25770088

An excellent book presenting the argument for evolutionary emotions is:

The Moral Animal: Why We Are, the Way We Are: The New Science of Evolutionary Psychology

By Robert Wright

It is very sobering and a little depressing, which with humans' natural hubris would drive most of the criticism of this work.

There are other very useful books on our genetic history. A wonderful popular summary by Nicholas Wade is:

Before the Dawn: Recovering the Lost History of Our Ancestors

And less interesting by him, but still worth reading:

A Troublesome Inheritance: Genes, Race and Human History

How Civilizations Die: (And Why Islam Is Dying Too)

By David Goldman and his excellent *"Spengler"* column also provide useful insights to these and a wide variety of topics.

References for *Human Evolution*

The History and Geography of Human Genes

By Luigi Luca Cavalli-Sforza et al is also a nice reference in this area giving valuable insight into how historical research through gene tracking can be examined.

The 10,000 Year Explosion: How Civilization Accelerated Human Evolution

By Gregory Cochran et al provides an interesting view into modern era evolutionary drivers.

References for *Evolutionary Emotions and What They Can Cause*

A review of an earlier book is also helpful in this chapter.

The Moral Animal: Why We Are, the Way We Are: The New Science of Evolutionary Psychology

By Robert Wright

To the extent that these predictions are validated and these explanations are useful, this might go a long way toward validating an evolutionary psychological perspective. These economic issues are longstanding holes in traditional economic theory. A better analytical comparison of the progeny gains from status leapfrogging compared to the risks taken in lotteries might go a long way to supporting the basic concepts of evolutionary psychology

A truly groundbreaking work by Reuven Brenner et al, **A World of Chance: Betting on Religion, Games, Wall Street**, contains some results from earlier papers with original research by the authors on gambling and especially lotteries. The research goes a long way toward forming a link between existing conundrums in economics to Evolutionary Psychology and has data that can be used to compare lottery gambling choices to genetic results in human's evolutionary environment. This book is highly recommended.

References for *Economy and Culture*

An Essay on the Principle of Population and Other Works by **Thomas Malthus**

Some Information about GDP per capita growth rates by country:

http://data.worldbank.org/indicator/NY.GDP.PCAP.KD.ZG

Some information on age and fertility

http://www.babycentre.co.uk/a6155/your-age-and-fertility

http://www.oecd.org/els/soc/47701118.pdf

http://www.prb.org/Publications/Articles/2008/muslimsineurope.aspx

ABOUT THE AUTHOR

Dennis Marx is a Pseudonym and Doesn't Exist. If he was a real person, however, he would have been a Fellow in the Society of Actuaries, a successful entrepreneur, as well as a sometimes physicist, and engineer working in missile navigation.

Printed in Great Britain
by Amazon

27667341R00066